SOCIAL
NATION

S O C I A L
NATION

HOW TO HARNESS THE POWER OF SOCIAL MEDIA TO ATTRACT CUSTOMERS, MOTIVATE EMPLOYEES, AND GROW YOUR BUSINESS

BARRY LIBERT

WILEY

John Wiley & Sons, Inc.

Contents

takes courage but pays off. Avoid the top 10 errors of going social.

EPILOGUE: Business and Social Become One 211

Creating a great family is like building a successful business. Set simple, clear principles. Offer guidelines; don't make demands. Let others interpret the guidelines to create greatness. Don't waste any more time. Join the Social Nation and benefit.

Preface

You make a living by what you get. You make a life by what you give.

—Winston Churchill

About 15 years ago my wife, Ellen, started asking me, "Why don't businesses get it?" She would come home from work, sit across the dinner table from me, and say, "Why don't they understand that organizations depend more on their communities, not their products and services, for enduring success?" At the time, she was the dean of students at Harvard Dental School and was troubled by the fact that students were not viewed as a community of contributors that could help reinvent the school, curriculum or fund raising activities.

"At Harvard, they spend a lot of time talking about how much money they have under management," Ellen would tell me. "They talk about how many buildings they own. They talk about the number of tenured faciulty, their research grants, and almost everything except the community of students and their interactions.

Ever since she said that to me, I've paid close attention to how organizations operate and what they really manage and measure— revenues from products and services versus information from customer and employee communities and their interactions. And the bottom line is that I realized Ellen was right.

Businesses cared more about assets and money, than they did people and their relationships. They couldn't remember the names of their customers and employees and didn't seem interested in creating friends with their constituents. They didn't treat these people as loyal fans, great friends, or true followers. Business weren't realizing the value they could actually generate with their help if they viewed them in this context. Simply put, I realized that businesses weren't living up to the age-old promise of putting the customer first. Further, companies and organizations weren't treating employees as the most important assets for driving growth.

Take Facebook, which was started at Harvard by a Harvard student to serve and connect the student community there. Although the students attended Harvard, the university didn't value the power of the social networks that were being created on campus. As a result, Harvard missed the opportunity to not only help their

students benefit from the friends and communities that were being created but also didn't help foster deep, ongoing relationships with those students networks post graduation.

In short, the result is that more than $10 billion of Facebook value was conceived at Harvard, by a Harvard student, to serve the Harvard student community (initially). Ultimately, the university missed out on fulfilling the students' needs and the economic benefit that followed. In fact, Harvard has little to do with a business that more than 500 million people today actively call their own personal nation.

Yet Harvard continues to say that its most important assets are its people (students, faculty, and donors), all the while doing little to foster their community using today's social technologies. Until recently, they didn't even understand that building their own on-line communities for their students and their parents, alumni, employees (including faculty), partners, and benefactors was critical to their future vitality.

I think I know why.

SEEN BUT NOT HEARD

Growing up, my parents, like many parents 50 years ago, taught me and my siblings that children should be "seen and not heard." Consequently, we sat silently at the dinner table each night listening to our parents. Night after night we basically learned that we were to live according to their beliefs and rules. They were in charge and we were not. The message was loud and clear.

My parents were no different from most parents of that generation in believing children were supposed to listen, follow orders, and do as they were told. The same was true for school. Teachers taught and the students were supposed to do little more than listen.

So, no surprise that this attitude has been translated into today's business world. Most of today's leaders were raised by parents who were similar to mine. Consequently, the clear reality of business today is that leaders believe they should lead, managers manage, and employees are supposed to follow. Essentially, employees are supposed to be seen, not heard.

In addition, business leaders haven't treated customers much differently. They tell them what to do: "Buy our products and services—and don't bother giving us feedback about what you've just bought, because we're too busy." Examples of this attitude are everywhere. Companies haven't taken us very seriously. As proof, they route our calls for support through automated systems, giving us little or no ability to reach a human. They haven't traditionally asked for or incorporated our feedback in their products or services. Instead, they tend to believe that they know best what we want.

Finally, they haven't modified their marketing and advertising programs to meet our needs. Instead, they broadcast what they have to sell the old-fashioned way, by bombarding us with their newest campaigns on TV, radio and in print, rather than engaging us in a two-way conversation. Clearly, if organizations thought about us as friends and followers, let alone fans, this is not the way they would conduct themselves.

HARVARD ISN'T ALONE

In the early 1990s, as my wife was just beginning to sound the "social alarm," I was working at

John Hancock, as a managing director in the firm's real estate department. Every day, I would ride up and down the elevators in one of the tallest buildings in Boston, past all the other floors. When I happened to ride the elevators with various Hancock executives, I would ask a few basic questions: "Who leases from us? What can we learn from all the people who work on each floor? How can we learn from them about what we should do to make our services better and more comprehensive?"

My questions generally would be met with blank stares. Nevertheless, I kept asking the questions. "We should be talking to these people, asking them what they want and how we can deliver it to them," I kept insisting. Sadly, however, I was the odd man out. "They are our tenants," I was told. "We are their landlord. They just rent space from us"

The Hancock executives reminded me of my parents because they thought tenants should be seen and not heard. They may have used different words, but the message was the same. The executives believed our tenants should occupy the  building on *our* terms, and therefore we didn't need to care about what they were doing or how they were doing other than provide space. As a result, Hancock failed to seize the opportunity to build a tenant nation—or a nation of residents, office occupants and retailers in which all of our tenants needs were met—and they became our loyal fans and followers.

I decided I couldn't stay in real estate. It was too inhuman an industry for me. I wanted to hear *from* people, not just lease them space in buildings. I truly wanted to understand their wants and needs, and give them a voice. More importantly, I wanted to understand how I could change what I was doing, based, at least in part, on their input. Finally, I believed that if businesses could convert customers and employees into friends, fans, and followers, real value could be created.

As a result of these experiences, in 1997, I proposed to write a book called *My Wife Is Right,* formulated on Ellen's simple premise that companies should focus increasingly on people, and their wants and needs—especially their emotional needs—and less on products and services. They should pay greater attention to the processes that made their communities of people feel important. Further more, I had been noticing, that with globalization, all products and services were becoming commoditized over time, and that the only enduring source of value for businesses was their communities of people.

With all this as background, I was becoming consumed with how little businesses knew about the social and networking aspects of their employees' and customers' lives. They definitely weren't paying attention to all of the relationships (friends, families, other connections) that were attached to the customers they served, and who, in turn, served them (employees). I saw clearly that each connection was an invitation to make another connection and form another relationship.

But businesses and their leaders didn't seem to get it.

Silly me. I thought I could actually write a book about my wife's observations. But publishers said, "No way." I was told that no one would read a book about some man's wife being right, or about how companies were the sum total of their community relationships. I was told that no one wanted to hear how leaders had to become more emotive and put other people and relationships first if they wanted to prosper. I was told to forget about it.

But I couldn't.

ALIGNING WITH MY CHILDREN

Around this time I was also paying attention to the changes in technology and communication as I watched my two sons grow up. When our children entered middle school, I realized that I wanted to be part of their lives. I wanted to spend less time on the road for work and more time at home. I wanted a career that would allow me to "travel" with my sons along their journey. More importantly, I wanted to be able do it according to their schedule, on their terms. In other words, I wanted to be with them when they woke up in the morning, go to work only after they had gone to school, attend their afternoon sports and extracurricular activities, eat dinner with them, and then go back to work when they were doing their homework. Finally, I wanted to become familiar with the technologies my kids were using to communicate with their peers so that I could communicate with them using the same tools. In essence, I wanted to live a life that aligned with their lives, and communicate in their words, while using their technologies in order to create our own family nation.

KAYAK.COM PURSUES A NEW WAY OF WORKING

Today, I'm hardly alone in wanting to connect my family and my business—on new, more social terms. Paul English, co-founder of Kayak.com, the travel search engine, has built into his day a very important ritual. He drives his 14-year-old son to school almost every single day. He schedules meetings and business travel around this simple yet important practice, and you can be sure that 20 years from now much of what binds them together will be memories from those early-morning car rides.

English conducts meetings at other people's desks. He goes to *them*. He sits with the product managers; he wants everyone to contribute, to add to the discussion. He also answers the customer support line personally, because he wants to hear directly from the people he's serving. He wants them to know him, and he

wants to know them. He had a bright red phone installed in the middle of the engineering department that rings when a customer service call is coming in. Not only does he expect his engineers to answer the phone and solve problems, but he does the same.

In all these ways, English puts himself in the middle of his community. He demonstrates that he's got his sleeves rolled up and is ready to work for his fans and followers. He leads by example. Like other leaders and companies that are joining the Social Nation, English understands that people want to be treated like individuals, not statistics. He understands customers count and human connections matter even more to Kayak's future.

MY FIRST SOCIAL NATION

Much like English, I realized that there was a way to connect the two parts of my life and build a company based on creating on-line communities. In June 2001, long before Facebook had even been conceived, I joined a start-up, financed by a Chicago-based private equity firm, to build online community software and service offerings for companies. The company had 20 customers and 9 employees, and its premise was simple: We were going to use the Web and telephones to enable call-center executives to share directly with one another what worked and what didn't. Our offerings were equally simple: We organized weekly and monthly Web conferences, captured our member's conversations and synthesized their insights, then made them available on-line for our members to hear and use in their daily activities.

How did this early approach to nation building come about? This Chicago based investor had embraced the idea that people had an absolute right to "be seen and heard." Further, they believed that all their interactions could and should be captured and made available to members to help them and their organizations make better decisions, faster based on the experiences of others. We named the organization—the Customer Care Strategy Forum

(CCSF), and its mission was the sharing of personal and professional experiences so that everyone in the community could benefit from each other.

CCSF morphed into Mzinga over time. Swahili for "beehive," Mzinga was named to capture the notion of combining collaboration and individual actions to create a socially successful organization. Mzinga is now located in Waltham, Massachusetts, a town about 15 miles outside Boston. Its mission is still to allow everyone to be seen and heard in the business world—employees, customers, partners, and investors, alike. We do this so that organizations can create friends, fans, and followers, the way Facebook has done for us in our personal lives so that they can learn from their communities of followers.

Our focus at Mzinga is on helping businesses build their connections with their employees and customers to build their own Social Nations. Another important goal at Mzinga is to convert the conversations of those friends, fans, and followers into actionable insights so that companies can benefit from the input of their customers and employees. Finally, we work hard to give customers and employees a voice in the design and direction of the companies they buy from and work for to enhance their loyalty.

To make that happen, we provide the social strategies, software, services, and analytic tools that organizations need so they can effectively listen to and hear their employees and customers feedback, while learning from their online interactions and communications. Currently, we manage and facilitate nearly 2 billion conversations a month, in more than 15,000 online communities, for more than 250 companies. In short, helping companies create friends, fans, and followers in on-line communities is what we do for a living. Through that process, businesses—and their leaders—find new ways to create value.

WHY READ THIS BOOK?

This book was written to help you and other members of your team, gain three critical capabilities:

1. Assess and learn about your social skills—a critical requirement in today's networked world;
2. Benefit from the 7 rules for building your own nation of fans, friends, and followers using social media so that you can create a community that cares about your organization and wants to help you grow and innovate; and
3. Provide you the steps to get started including the 10 pitfalls to avoid.

Over the last nine years, I have experienced directly and qualitatively the value of the social revolution, in the form of happier, more involved customers and employees; improved products and services; greater revenues and higher profits; and better investor relations. This book will help you master the principles for social success as it shows you how to avoid the pitfalls along the journey of refocusing your company on your future— your community, their insights and contributions.

Enjoy the read, then join the community of readers like yourself to discuss what works and what doesn't. Become a part of the conversation surrounding today's Social Revolution, at www .socialnationbook.com. I look forward to hearing your thoughts—and so will others. See you there.

PART 1

THE FUTURE OF BUSINESS IS SOCIAL

The trouble with most of us is that we know too much that ain't so.

—Mark Twain

1

SOCIAL MEDIA CREATES REAL VALUE

". . . dependence is the paradigm of you—you take care of me; you come through for me; you didn't come through; I blame you for the results. Independence is the paradigm of I—I can do it; I am responsible; I am self-reliant; I can choose. Interdependence is the paradigm of we—we can do it; we can cooperate; we can combine our talents and abilities and create something greater together."

—Stephen Covey

In May 2010, GlaxoSmithKline opened to the public the designs behind chemical compounds that have been experimented with as a drug for treating malaria. Traditionally guarded with information and formulas, this company and the pharmaceutical industry in general has officially made the move toward a community-based model. Essentially, Glaxo is relying on a community of interested parties to find the cures that they haven't yet found.

Ultimately, by making this change, they are saying their approach to research and product development will be more successful, more powerful, and probably less expensive, by relying on a community of people who don't work for them. Their belief—by opening their doors to others, better things can happen. This open-source drug development approach, as radical as it may seem today in such a traditional and closed industry, illustrates Glaxo's trust in the power of the power of a community of interested parties, to achieve the innovative results it seeks.

For them, it's a new and social way of doing research, inventing drugs, and solving health care problems around the world. It's also a signal to other major companies that the time has come to accept the fact that social media has the potential of creating real, measurable value.

Consequently, this example shows that being social does not just mean being on Facebook or Twitter. Nor is it only about connecting with your friends at work to share what movie you are seeing or what you are eating for lunch. That's a part of the social media craze, but not all of it. For them, it means using social networks and technologies media to connect with people on an emotional and individual level so that your company can innovate and grow. Facebook and Twitter are part of the equation, but they won't build your community of fans or generate followers for you without your own time and effort to solve the hard problems that create value in your organization—that's not their job; that's your job.

This book is about your company. You've already spent time and effort building your brand, products, and services along with your customers, employees and investors. Consequently, it's your job to use social media to engage your customers in ways that they've never been engaged, motivate your employees in ways they've never been inspired and innovate in ways you never imagined, Today's social media technologies will allow you to accomplish your goals faster, better, and cheaper than ever before. And they can help you create value in ways that are meaningful and rewarding to you and your constituents.

BUILDING YOUR OWN SOCIAL NATION

For the past 200 years (starting with the Industrial Revolution) making business nonsocial was what organizations were all about. Businesses weren't looking to create social communications with constituents at a personal or individual level. In fact, business was about making money at any and all costs, while dehumanizing the personal elements of our daily lives.

For example, the old rules of business suggested that we shouldn't take it personally when we were fired, received bad service, bought inferior products, or earned unexpectedly poor financial results. Further, businesses often still hide behind the motto, "Don't take it personally; it's just business." And they get away with it because we know, and they know, that we, as individuals, don't count.

But all that is changing. Your employees and your customers want to be engaged on a very personal level, and not just through a yearly survey or at an annual conference. And if you choose not to engage with them, they will do it without you anyway – and you don't want that.

So, how can you become a part of those social conversations and interactions? How can you benefit from what they are saying and to whom they are saying it? Simply: You can join the Social Nation revolution and make it your priority and your company's strategy to go social. Ultimately, this book is intended to serve as a guide that can help you convert your customers and employees to fans and followers to achieve your true potential.

Today, we—as employees, partners, and customers—are telling companies what to make, market, and sell. According to a report released September 23, 2009, by the Nielsen Company, the amount of time spent on the Internet in the previous year had increased substantially reflecting our interest in two way communications with each other and the organizations that serve us. The study revealed the following:

- *We* spent 17 percent of our online time social networking or blogging.
- *We* spent 83 percent more time in online social networks than the year prior.

- *We* are driving advertisers to spend an expected $2.6 billion on these social sites by 2012.

The statistics illustrate that companies need to increasingly turn to social media to change what they do and how they do it just as Glaxo has. The reason they need to is because they have to capture the voices of their employees and customers if they want to innovate. At the same time, customers and employees want to impact every aspect of your business. They want to have an impact on all types of companies—small or large, local or national. People who have never before been asked to contribute to business now want to share their opinions, criticisms, and praise with you. And they want to share these thoughts, and perspectives among themselves, as well.

Building your social nation means changing what you think it means to build a company. This emerging social era is about engaging everyone around you to redefine what you do and how you do it—including sales, marketing, R&D, customer support, and product development (see Chapter 11 for more details). Examples of this are everywhere. Customers (not the businesses) want to decide where we should eat. For this reason, Open Table has created a Dining Nation. Amazon has created a Readers Nation for everyone who wants to determine the books you should read. Travel Nation helps to determine which hotel we should book thanks to Trip Advisor. Investor Nation steers us toward the stocks we should buy (TheStreet .com).

And it does not stop there. People want to have a say in which products companies should design and sell (Proctor & Gamble). Jet Blue has built True Blue Nation to develop loyal travelers. These and many other companies are all beginning to understand the power of creating friends, fans, and followers to build their business.

BENEFITTING FROM THE CONTRIBUTION OF OTHERS

Here's the exciting part of building your own Social Nation. We, all of the individuals that constitute your crowd of interested participants, want to help. We can show you how you can benefit from all of our input as you seek to build your nation. But to do that, you have to hear our voices and embrace what we're saying, while working hard to establish meaningful relationships with us. This is how businesses can avoid the fate of companies such as GM. This book will guide you through the steps to change what you do and how you do it, based on a new way of thinking about your company, in order to profit from today's Social Nation movement. This means creating extraordinary organizations and value based on the input of others.

Social Nation was not written to tell you how to use Facebook and Twitter. Facebook and Twitter have already built their own nation of friends and are benefiting from them. Rather, this book is about helping you first define and then build your own Social Nation with today's social media tools (see Chapter 11). Further, *Social Nation* is about developing new skills you will need to reap the benefits of participating in today's social order it's also about new open, organizational designs, and

ways to innnovate; and it's about new ways of
rewarding others. Finally, this book is about how you,
as an individual, can improve your social self to
benefit from this Social Revolution that is influencing
all of us.

SOCIAL NATIONS WILL BECOME THE DOMINANT FORCE IN BUSINESS

All of us know that social interactions already play a
dominant role in our personal lives, but so far they
have played a recessive role in the business realm.
While our online interactions have increased in our
personal lives, most businesses still believe that
social interactions and interests should be left
behind when we go to the office. "Be seen and not
heard" remains the adage that still applies to much
of the working world. That's because organizations
are built to be impenetrable and dictatorial entities
that create, manufacture, promote, and sell products
or services based on the insights of the few about
what the many want.

The proof is there for us all to see. We've spent
time and money building huge industrial corporations
such as General Electric, Microsoft, and 3M. We've
created massive institutions such as Harvard and
Yale; we've endowed them, poured money into them,
and made their brands larger than life. These
institutions became the foundation of our society.
They became our voice. But they have fallen short of
having built communities we can call ours—like
Facebook or Twitter—where our voices are heard
and our interactions matter.

However, social technology and the networks they
create are enabling all organizations to join in. It

enables everyone to share and offer ideas. It offers everyone an opportunity to be leaders and real participants in their own right, contributing ideas and comments. As people share and interact and create communities, their voices are becoming more powerful. In turn, businesses are being forced to listen to their collective desires, ideas, and perspectives and respond. The good news is that the most successful enterprises of our future are going to incorporate our voices into everything they do and make.

EMBRACING YOUR SOCIAL NATION TO BENEFIT

Creating your own Social Nation may seem daunting, and in many regards even unappealing because you may not want to give everyone a voice. Maybe you still think that the business and social worlds should be separate from one another. And maybe you think your customers don't know what they want. So it's not surprising to find that while some companies are ready to become part of the Social Nation, others are wary, and still others remain unwilling.

There are three types of companies out there right now. The first group consists of those that don't know what it means to build their own Social Nation. These companies are reluctant to become social because their perception is that doing so won't produce any additional economic value. The second group is trying to be social and build on-line communities but doesn't quite know how to get started and how they can benefit. The third group includes organizations that have already built strong social nations (such as *American Idol*, Cisco, Procter & Gamble) and are looking to make social pervasive throughout their organizations, to enhance everything they do.

Regardless of which group you and your organization fall into, this book can work for you and your team. Building your Social Nation requires that you share your team's personal experiences and connections with others to produce results for you, your family, and your organization. It means integrating your work and life experiences, and it means connecting the two separate parts of your life into a seamless whole. In the world of Social Nations, our work and personal worlds meld, as our formerly disparate values for each become one. This is the foundation that will ultimately separate the merely good companies from the successful ones, and the successful ones from those that are truly extraordinary.

FOUR DRIVING FORCES

There are four major forces driving the shift toward a more social business world:

1. Today's Changing Workforce
2. Open Business Models
3. Emerging Technologies
4. Social Monitoring and Measurement Tools

First, people are becoming agitated; they want a voice in the commercial world. They want businesses to hear them, whether they are employees or customers. Second, once fiercely guarded, closed business models are becoming more open. Companies, like Glaxo, are relying on others for ideas, innovation, and new revenues. Third, advances in technology have exploded at an unprecedented speed and capacity. This has enabled the voice of the public to be heard, relationships to be formed, and open source models to be implemented in industries, that will forever change the face of business. Fourth, new social intelligence is measuring our needs and sentiments before we realize we even have them.

The Workforce Is Becoming Social

Forty years ago, about one-third of the workforce was female; today, women are on the verge of outnumbering men. Simply, the "who" in the business world has changed, and continues to change. According to a 2009 *Time* magazine poll, 40 percent of women are the primary earners in their household, and 84 percent still believe that business hasn't done enough to address the needs of the modern family.[1]

In today's business world, people from around the globe are sharing their opinions and expertise. Young people, if not college students, are creating companies that produce extraordinary value. Minorities and recent immigrants are starting online business sensations. Thus, business is fast becoming less of a closed society and increasingly open to everyone.

The fastest-growing segment of Facebook users is made up of people 35 or older. In November 2009, according to Google's Ad Planner, a site that tracks web traffic, on 84 percent of social networking sites women, not men, are the most frequent users.

---

[1] Nancy Gibbs, "What Women Want Now," *Time*, October 14, 2009.

Women have always been the connectors, the relaters, and the conversation drivers. They bring a new voice into whatever they do; and since they now nearly dominate the workplace, they are bringing their personal values with them there, too.

Moms control more than 80 percent of household spending, which means they not only respond to advertising or marketing, but they write their own reviews and create discussion forums and blogs to keep each other informed. BlogHer, a site for women who blog, and that hosts more than 15 million users each month, is just one example of how far-reaching and powerful these voices can be when given the technology to enable them.

The crowd, moreover, has grown impatient as well as empowered, and no longer is willing to wait for businesses to catch up to their needs and demands. Currently, two-thirds of all people using social networking for business purposes are doing so through their own initiatives, rather than corporate-sponsored ones. In the emerging social World, the crowd is already ahead of business.

Business Models Are Becoming Open

The second reason businesses are becoming more social is that the traditional models are changing. *Crowd sourcing* has become increasingly popular and profitable. Crowds of people who don't work for you are creating new products and services for your competitors. Businesses, in turn, have to enable voices and offer rewards if they want to benefit from free lance contributors. Closed-models aren't disappearing overnight, but the open-source ones like Glaxo is pursuing are becoming more prevalent.

In order to embrace these new open organizational models of innovation and growth, companies need to embrace new ways of conducting research and generating sales and marketing messages. This does not mean replacing everything you already do well with something new. Instead, becoming an open business means integrating your community, into the successful elements you already have. By doing so, you will be able to monetize and capitalize on the collective voices and insights of others from which the best and brightest concepts will emerge.

Market research firm Gartner Inc. released key predictions for IT organizations on January 31, 2008, predicting that by 2012, 80 percent of commercial software will have open-source components. Companies are finding that they can use both internal employees, who are responsible for developing new models, while also relying on outside innovators, customers, and partners to create new opportunities. This new open-model makes it possible to reduce costs, slash time-to-market for new products and create new revenues faster than before, organically. What does all this mean? That businesses are no longer the gatekeepers of their own brands—their communities are.

Emerging Technologies Are Becoming Social

Enabling these more open business models are new technologies called Web 2.0. In the past, we had to buy expensive plane tickets or take long car rides to connect with family or attend annual college reunions. Now, we can connect in a matter of seconds with family, friends, and colleagues, as well as like-minded strangers who share our political interests, hobbies, or ailments. We can show that we care and share almost constantly with very little planning or travel costs. And we can interact on-line with people we know and those we don't to produce powerful new voices.

Further, Technology also allows business to reach people on *their* terms. As people become more and more comfortable engaging in personal online interactions—such as Twitter, Facebook, and other the new Web 2.0 tools—including blogs, discussion forums, instant chat, they are also beginning to engage with businesses and organizations in this way, as well. Even the U.S. Army is using social media to reach potential recruits. Knowing that younger generations are most effectively reached through new media, the Army is relying on blogging to make contact with future soldiers.

The social era is about embracing your audience in the way they want to be embraced. Ultimately, trying to resist social interactions and communications in business will prove to be futile. Trying to control it won't work, either. In contrast, empowering your customers and your employees to join you, in an authentic and responsible way, will lead to greater growth and value, from the friends, fans, and followers you create in all of your daily interactions.

Monitoring and Measurement Is Becoming Social

Behind the first three driving forces are systems that measure our contributions, quantify our sentiment, and provide companies with real intelligence about our current and future needs. These technologies, collectively referred to as *social intelligence*, is functioning behind the scenes of the most valuable companies to help organizations predict our behavior and respond to our needs. That said, it's no longer enough to just create more products or services. You can build a company around great products, but they alone won't be enough to connect your customers emotively or socially which is essential in today's highly competitive world.

In other words, it's not enough that technologies are enabling social interactions. Rather, leaders have to understand our sentiments and act on those requirements. In addition, emerging leaders have to embrace the understanding that to build friends, fans and followers they have to be emotionally and socially connected to us in ways never before contemplated.

ITS TIME TO EMBRACE YOUR SOCIAL SELF

Change is hard. Change takes sacrifice. Change requires today's leaders to give up some of what they're used to having and what they believe makes them so good at what they do, such as traditional transaction skills, acquisition skills, and managerial skills. These skills are no longer sufficient to be successful, however. Fortunately, we all have other skills, derived from our personal lives that we can, and must, call upon to assist us in succeeding in the Social Revolution.

The benefit of using these new social skills in your business is clear. This social movement allows organizations to receive real time feedback about how you are meeting your constituents' needs. This is one reason why customer and employee social networks are becoming increasingly popular. Leading companies and executives are discovering that these networks add value.

For example, Nike offers nine distinct networks that enable Latinos, the disabled, and Native American employees (to name just three) to convene around culture, specified needs, or contributions. Nike understands that a wealth of unstructured knowledge and information is being exchanged in these social networks by giving up control. The company is excited to learn from this phenomenon. Fortunately, Nike is not alone: more and more companies are catching on and building their communities of loyalists.

BEST BUY BUYS IN—AND BENEFITS

Take Best Buy. Several years ago, Steve Bendt and Gary Koelling were hired by the mega electronic retailer to develop advertising campaigns. They began by talking to the employees of Best Buy to get a sense of what customers were after in the stores. From this effort, they ended up with an entire internal employee network of engaged individuals, each of whom wanted to share knowledge, converse with one another, and hatch new ways of doing things. They named this network Blue Shirt Nation, after the recognizable color of the uniform worn by Best Buy employees.

Blue Shirt Nation has been an incredible success ever since. Within a year, 20,000 of the 150,000 employees had joined. Soon people were sharing everything from customer insights to photos of their cats. The network remains a keystone of the company's culture, proving that its executives trust their employees, not only to behave responsibly within Blue Shirt Nation but also to make recommended changes on policies, products, and services. Blue Shirt Nation has given each and every Best Buy employee a legitimate voice in the company.

BUILDING YOUR SOCIAL NATION TRANSLATES INTO GROWTH

As businesses adopt the notion that their customers and employees can help them achieve their needs, revenues and profitability will increase. A 2009 study by the University of Massachusetts–Dartmouth revealed that the companies willing to adopt social media will grow faster than those that do not engage in the new technologies.[2]

Significant and sustained engagement in social media is driving profitability. According to a study released by Wetpaint and Altimeter Group, financial performance increased by as much 18 percent on average in one year for those companies most engaged in social media. By comparison, those companies least engaged saw an average decline of 6 percent in revenues during the same period.[3]

In the past, companies and institutions have traditionally focused exclusively on the bottom line, while disregarding the people and the processes by which they got there. In today's social world, the

[2] Nora Ganim Barnes and Eric Mattson, "The Fortune 500 and Social Media: A Longitudinal Study of Blogging and Twitter Usage by America's Largest Companies," Center for Market Research at the University of Massachusetts, Dartmouth.
[3] "The World's Most Valuable Brands. Who's Most Engaged?" ENGAGEMENTdb, July 2009.

collective voice is driving business, leading to the conclusion that to reach that bottom line successfully, business must understand and embrace these social models, sensibilities, and processes.

WHAT'S NEXT?

This chapter introduced you to the benefit of creating a Social Nation of your own as Glaxo, Nike, and Best Buy are. Chapter 2 will describe the new social skills you need to develop to participate in the social revolution engulfing our society.

In Chapter 3, you will be introduced to the Social Quotient test, an online social skills assessment that will enable you to objectively and scientifically test your social capabilities. This test, designed by a group of scientists, specifically measures areas in which you are socially competent, and, for the first time lets you scientifically assess your social readiness and skills. This exciting tool will give you a concrete understanding of where you are currently on the social spectrum and what you can do to enhance your own—and your company's—social competencies.

The chapters comprising Part 2 of *Social Nation* detail, in turn, the seven prescriptions for achieving success and financial rewards in this new business era. We reveal the importance of engaging others around you in every way possible so as to achieve your company's full potential. These chapters cover leadership skills, social monitoring and measurement and new approaches to financial rewards that will help you achieve your organizational goals.

The book concludes with a guide on how to get started—tomorrow—by offering practical steps you can take, and pointing out 10 pitfalls you will want to avoid. In short, it illustrates that the sooner you build your own Social Nation, the sooner you will realize your personal and professional aspirations and reap the rewards that come from doing so.

SEVEN STEPS THAT START WITH YOU

The following is a preview of the seven guiding principles for implementing a successful social nation strategy at your company.

Principle 1: Develop Your Social Skills. Social leaders in the Social Nation are expected to follow more than they lead, while continuing to provide structure and support.

Principle 2: Let Culture Lead Your Way. When building your Social Nation, remember that culture is very important, so let your guiding principle be an open and honest environment.

Principle 3: Mind Your Online and Offline Manners. How you say something, versus what you say, be it online or off, will make a big difference in helping you to engage fans, friends, and followers.

Principle 4: Monitor, Measure and Adopt to Your Community's Needs. Social intelligence enables your company to monitor and measure everything that is happening around you—including the number and sentimennt of the conversations of your constituents—allowing you to modify what you do and how you do it.

Principle 5: Include Others in Everything You Do. As an organization that is seeking to benefit from building a Social Nation, you must rely on others in every part of your company. That is the only way to generate new revenues and increase profits.

Principle 6: Rely on Others for Growth and Innovation. Friends, fans, and followers are instrumental in achieving growth in today's connected world. Engaging all of your constituents is essential to building new products and services that matter.

Principle 7: Reward Others and You Will Be Rewarded, Too. As organizations focus more intently on making connections and building relationships, they want to be rewarded emotionally as well as financially. Successful businesses have to meet both needs.

Before beginning your journey toward implementing a successful social media strategy in your organization, you'll have an opportunity to assess your social skills. By defining what makes a leader great in today's open business environment we can help you discern how social you are and how you can better understand yourself and your team's readiness for today's realities.

PUT SOCIAL TO WORK FOR YOU—NOW

Now is the time to make everything—your strategy your skills, and your measurement systems—social. Given that we are by nature social beings, do we really have any other choice but to make our world more social? All you need now is to understand the social competencies you already have and use every day in your personal life, and then embrace the seven principles of social success outlined in the coming chapters. After that, you'll be well on your way to making whatever you do part of the new social business era.

2

WHY SOCIAL SKILLS MATTER

Every person I have known who has been truly happy has learned how to serve others.
—Albert Schweitzer

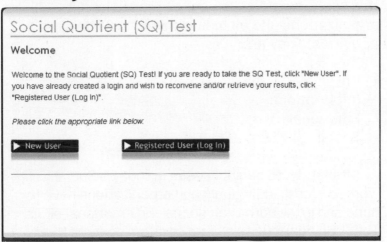

MƵinga

Social Quotient (SQ) Test

Welcome

Welcome to the Social Quotient (SQ) Test! If you are ready to take the SQ Test, click "New User". If you have already created a login and wish to reconvene and/or retrieve your results, click "Registered User (Log In)".

Please click the appropriate link below.

▶ New User   ▶ Registered User (Log In)

Only a few leaders understand all of the skills that are necessary to build a company in today's social world. We've been trained in other skills that have been necessary to build companies that were created in another age. In order to evolve from yesterday's skills to today's social competencies we have to understand where we've come from and how much work we have yet to do.

Agrarian workers and leaders had to develop certain skills that made them successful in that era. But once the Industrial Revolution came along, new skills were needed and people had to adapt accordingly and learn new competencies. Likewise, today's organizations need to think and act differently in order to successfully learn and adopt social skills to use in our connected world. Simply put, there are different skills for different ages and we can't merely transport one set of skills into the next age.

We've identified the four basic skills that define the four ages. These *strengths,* as we call them in this book, are used, in varying proportions, by all organizations and all individuals in their daily activities. They are:

- Physical
- Informational
- Emotional
- Social

Ultimately, to be successful in today's Socially Networked World, individuals and organizations have to hone and grow both their social and emotional skills. They can continue to rely on or retain some of their physical and informational talents, but not as dominant skills. For a better understanding of the differences in each of these skills and why social is the emerging skill for today's age, let's take a look back at history.

DIFFERENT SKILLS FOR DIFFERENT AGES

For centuries, business was about making things. In the beginning, we were farmers. Brute strength was required to till the farm. Then came the industrial age and we all labored on manufacturing lines. Then came the information age in which information was the dominant strength.

In time, as our way of life migrated from the agrarian and industrial to an age of information and intellect, with it emerged new strengths and competencies, for example in software development. Along with those new skills, new sources of value were created, such as

companies that could monetize information, or
software firms that could create code. Their
employees and their customers benefitted, as well.
More recently, with the Social Revolution well
underway, companies have been forming emotional
connections with their communities, to ensure that
they motivate strong fans and followers. It is those
organizations, and their leaders who understand this
transformation in focus, that have begun to prosper
directly because of these relationships.

In today's Social World all four of these skills—
physical, informational, emotional, and social—are
essential, although the scale is tipping quickly in
favor of social strengths. In fact, companies and
leaders will increasingly need to recruit people who
understand what it takes to generate the loyalty of
fans, friends, and followers in order to succeed.
These future leaders will have the skills and
capabilities to build vibrant communities as the
foundations of their companies.

This is not to suggest that you can't or won't
succeed if you are strong in physical or informational
skills, for example, and not social ones. It does
mean, however, that reaping the maximum benefits
from the Social Nation and the value it can generate
for your company will require mastering your social
competencies. To further illustrate the benefit of and
need for social skills and relationships in the social
era, let's look at each strength in the order in which
they emerged and were adopted by businesses.

PHYSICAL STRENGTHS

Individuals or organizations driven by Physical
Strengths (PS) relied upon hard work and tactical

execution to make things and meet the concrete demands of their businesses. They are singularly focused on production, and less in touch with the needs, desires, or feelings of their employees and customers. How their constituents are "feeling" or what they are looking to achieve as individuals is not central to their thinking.

Individuals driven by Physical Strengths (PS) are typically intent on getting the job done, meeting deadlines, and hitting targets. The overriding motto of PS leaders could be summed up as, "Just work hard and good things happen." PS leaders thrive on operating according to rules, policies, and procedures marked by clear directions; they typically dislike organizations, models, and economies that are prone to change. Their core skills tend to be limited to specialized and repeated task execution within a limited range of expertise. Their scope of control is based on what they can physically produce, build, or sell. Thus, PS-led companies dominate primarily through size, volume, and output.

Ford Works Hard, Physically, to Make Cars Better

Consider Alan Mulally, who has degrees in aeronautical and astronautical engineering. Needless to say, he knows how to build things. He also has a master's degree in management from the Massachusetts Institute of Technology Sloan School of Management. And while he was an executive at Boeing Commercial Airplanes, Mulally was largely credited when the company gained an edge over competitor Airbus in the mid-2000s. He is known for turning Boeing into one of the best-run manufacturing companies in the world.

One part engineer and one part businessman, Mulally was hired in 2006 as CEO of the Ford Motor Company (a Mzinga client) by the founder's grandson, Bill Ford. Ford and his board asked Mulally to transfer his manufacturing skills from airplanes to cars, with the hope that he could help their floundering company prosper. He accepted the challenge.

Mulally is a hard worker. He lives about three miles from Ford's global headquarters in Dearborn, Michigan, arrives at his office  each day by 5:15 AM, and often works for at least 12 hours, if not more. He's a dedicated man.

Even as the entire U.S. auto industry was collapsing, and getting bailed out by the government, Mulally set about restructuring Ford's business without federal support. He has worked hard to bring back once-popular brands, such as the Taurus, primarily by focusing on the company's physical capabilities. As a result, today, Ford is again beginning to make exceptional vehicles of which the founding family would be proud.

In January 2010, *Auto Week* named Ford's next-generation Focus the "most significant" vehicle of the year; *Motor Trend* named the Ford Focus the Car of 2010. Citing the vehicle's exceptional fuel economy, advanced driving quality, and high-performance four-cylinder engines, reviews overall for the new Taurus have been glowing. Increasingly, there is little doubt that what made Ford great in the first place—hard work that produced tangible things (cars)—is the direction in which the company is again headed to ensure its long-term future success.

INFORMATIONAL STRENGTHS

The Informational Strengths (IS) competency is new, developed since the advent of the computer chip. This skill is based on the organization and dissemination of knowledge. IS employees, leaders, and companies grew out of the mid-1950s and believe that the way to create value is to work smarter, versus harder, by improving efficiency and production through the transfer of knowledge to others. They accomplished this by relying on technology and by writing the software that enabled the production of information.

Becoming more fluent in informational competencies initially meant focusing on documentation, training, and analytics, rather than physical capabilities. This new skill, using information, allowed leaders and their companies— many in the services industries—to capture greater value using less capital than their industrial or agrarian brethren.

Thomson Reuters Succeeds at Selling Information

Roy Thomson started his career in 1934 as publisher of Ontario's *Timmins Daily Press*; he was a man who "owned information." In 1953, he acquired the *Scotsman* and moved to that country, where he continued to acquire newspapers and sell newspapers. Eventually he moved into publishing when he bought Sweet & Maxwell, in 1987. In 1996, the Thomson Corporation doubled in size when the company bought West Publishing, best known for its legal research division, Westlaw.

Then, in February 2000, in a surprising move, Thomson announced that it was selling more than 120 of its papers, to enable the company to  turn its attention to online holdings. The company was widely criticized at the time for following what was possibly only a fad (technology). Thompson's decision to sell of most of its newspapers was made quickly, and was a bold move, to be sure; but it was also one of the most forward-thinking tactics an information company like Thomson could have made at the time. Thomson had decided to focus, almost exclusively, on the electronic information and delivery business.

Eight years later, in 2008, Thomson merged with Reuters, another information giant. Thomson Reuters, as the business has since been known, describes itself as "the world's leading source of intelligent information for businesses and professionals." The company now successfully provides massive amounts of information through online distribution channels.

More specifically, the company profitably implements technology to capture, collate, and distribute extraordinary, highly desirable information that is accessed by millions of people, 24 hours a day. And because the content is available online and via mobile devices, Thomson Reuters helps people and businesses make better decisions, faster. In addition, the company understands the changing behaviors of its consumers and responds accordingly by making its offerings (information) available to them in a way that makes the most sense.

EMOTIONAL STRENGTHS

Both individuals and organizations develop Emotional Strengths (ES) in order to create symbiotic relationships to bring about a mutual benefit and value. As employees become more diversified, and the economy more global, ES companies and leaders make emoting and sensing capabilities central to their organizations' development. In fact, over the last decade or so, employees, customers, and partners have been demanding greater value through personal attention, flexibility, and shared rewards.

By listening, empathizing, and making personal connections, ES-enabled leaders motivate their teams and customers to work together to accomplish even more. They capture the hearts and minds of their communities through these emotional connections and communication venues. They also leverage emotive skills such as compassion, caring, and mentoring.

As we all are bombarded by untold amounts of information, and overwhelmed by competing responsibilities, more and more of us seek to bond with one another through technologies such as email, texting, and cell phones; but this causes the line between our personal and business lives to blur.

Yes, technology has enabled us to make these personal and emotional connections more easily,

which has also made them more important to us,
even in business. However, this skill, and its
development in organizations, is still new and not yet
fully understood; nor has it been fully embraced
universally. Many companies and their leaders
continue to regard these skills as "too soft." Those
companies that are adding emotional capabilities,
however, are creating new business models that are
showing real, positive results—whether for single
divisions of large organizations or as the core
premise and capability of start-ups.

Bubbe Nourishes Hearts and Minds

Being emotional is about connecting to the
individual and personal needs and responses of
the people around you. For Bayla Sher, this means
cooking and sharing recipes with her online
followers and viewers.
Sher, who goes by
the moniker "Bubbe"
(Yiddish for
"grandmother"),
works from an
outdated kitchen and
follows retro recipes,
and only recently
learned about email
and the Internet.
Nevertheless, along with her grandson Avrom
Honig, this 80-something grandmother from
Worcester, Massachusetts, started an online
cooking show called "Feed Me Bubbe." Part
kitsch, part nostalgia, Bubbe makes her fans feel
all warm and fuzzy inside, reminding them of their

own grandmas, complete with her good and not-so-good recipes.

Along with recipes, fun, and a show that's inviting to multiple generations, Bubbe sells emotion. According to her Web site, "Feed Me Bubbe" has three goals: to provide a simple, easy-to-understand recipe, share a Yiddish word of the day, and give followers "the feeling of going to your grandmother's."

Sher could be selling cars, but she happens to be demo-ing kosher recipes. What really matters is how her viewers feel. Judging by the emails and letters she receives from all over the world, they feel great, and want more. They want to connect with her, hear from her, write to her, and ask her advice.

SOCIAL STRENGTHS

Individuals who have Social Strengths (SS) take emotional competencies one giant step further: They seek to apply listening, sensitivity, and emotive skills to their entire business network of friends, fans, and followers to build enduring and vibrant communities. In a socially networked world, a social professional understands that the power is shifting to the crowd, and he or she becomes a facilitator and learns to follow. The leader becomes the person in the back of the room, not the front.

Being socially competent means that you understand at a fundamental level that to have a successful business you must focus on everyone else, and their needs, not yours. Being socially competent also means that you act on this understanding. Compare this to the Emotional Strengths world, in which the goal is to satisfy both your needs and the other person's needs.

Socially enabled leaders are self-actualized; they humble themselves to the social network they serve and are coordinating and motivating. They are comfortable being emotive and sensing; they facilitate constituents interactions. That is not to say that high-performing SS individuals are passive bystanders. Not at all. They passionately and purposefully orchestrate others actions, while enabling open, honest conversations and interactions. They are willing to take personal emotional and social risks, be transparent, and be held accountable to their employees, customers, and partners.

Socially competent leaders and individuals are also explorers, in that they are comfortable navigating uncharted territory, seeking to merge their business and social worlds. Nonetheless, they are confident that the old ways of doing things won't work in today's socially networked world, and are willing to take the risks inherent with all change.

TopCoder Relies on Their Community

Take TopCoder: Brothers Robert and Jack Hughes were at the helm of a successful software consulting business when they realized that they were wasting a lot of time and money on finding good talent. They were constantly looking for gifted software developers, and recognized they were too often getting bogged down in resume reviews and interviews. They also saw how many unqualified developers were moving into the industry.

So the brothers decided to develop a contest as a way to lure the truly talented. It would serve two purposes: To give them a pool of people to pick from, and allow talented developers to "strut their stuff." These competitions—in everything from algorithms, design, development, and more—caught on, and by 2001 the brothers had launched TopCoder.com.

The company's clients are now the *reason* for the competitions. TopCoder's clients in turn rely on people all over the world to solve their problems, create their software, and influence their businesses. This is, pure and simple, a Social Strengths way of doing business, one that relies on the crowd and puts trust in the crowd.

The company's competitions also offer an opportunity for developers to create and design in real time. In essence, the Hughes brothers have taken a technical discipline and turned it into a sport, all the while serving a clear business need. They understand the value of leveraging technology to connect lots of developers to solve lots of problems. Ultimately, they realized that the best way to develop software was not to hire more people, but to build a social network that enabled anyone and everyone to code software they could then make available to the highest bidder.

PUTTING THE FOUR STRENGTHS IN CONTEXT

The following figure maps the four strengths— physical, informational, emotional, and social—as a guide for how to think about your skills (and your personal) key strengths. It can be helpful for determining which skills your organization predominantly values and which one it lacks or underappreciates. It can even help you to think about

Four Types of Organizational Strengths

#	Strengths Type	Core Characteristics	Focus	Organization	External Environment
1	Physical	Hard work	Tactical execution and production	Hierarchical and bureaucratic	Traditional and well-defined
2	Informational	Smart work	Analytical and interpretive	Structured and organized	Newer and less structured
3	Emotional	Emotional connections	Coaching, connecting and partnership	Personal and connected	Emerging and loosely defined
4	Social	Social networking	Listening, anticipating, enabling and facilitating	Networked, and self-organized	Unstructured and undefined

how to chart your own personal development to generate greater value.

Remember, having friends, fans, and followers in your business can help you create new products, generate higher revenues, encourage more invigorated customers and employees, and, thereby, boost profits. Having and using the skills to develop relationships with people who will stand by you is crucial to business success. You can't get there if you are focused on creating products and services while lacking the skills that result in enduring personal and real relationships.

GETTING COMFORTABLE WITH YOUR SOCIAL SELF

Many individuals, leaders, and companies have begun to make significant strides to build their social strengths. But they still face significant obstacles and challenges before they can entirely embrace these emotional and social skills. Traditional thinkers remain stuck in thinking that only physical and informational strengths or assets will create value. These obstacles often are connected to their perception of controlling risk. What they don't understand is that in this socially networked world the only way to control risk is to join the conversation.

Making you and your company social means embracing these new strengths, if you want to benefit from the capabilities and contributions of your community. It also means relinquishing control to your constituents, if you expect to benefit from your latent social networks. In the end, companies and their leaders will realize that they need to harness all four strengths—physical, informational, emotional, and social—to build their organization. In other words, a company is the sum total of its people, processes, and skills. That said, and for the foreseeable future, social leaders will produce the most value as the world becomes increasingly open and connected.

While working hard and producing physical things will continue to be important, this approach will not be as valuable as working smart and delivering information. The same is true for emotive connections and social networking. Each of these organizational strengths reflects the era in which the business was built. To put this in context, consider that Henry Ford created his business at the inception of the last century, whereas Thomson was started midway through that century. More recent phenomena are emotionally connected and socially networked organizations such as Zappos and Kayak, which were built by embracing newer social skills, processes and technologies.

As we enter an era when anyone can make any product, and we can all interact and communicate on an equal basis, what will increasingly matter is our ability to connect emotionally and socially with our constituents. It's this emotional and social connection that we can use to construct the social networks that are powerful, aligned, and fast-moving.

START TO BUILD YOUR SOCIAL CAPABILITIES

Look at your company, board of directors, team, and partnerships to assess where you are with regard to the four competencies, then determine how far you have to go before you achieve social nirvana. Consider who is working for you, and what skills he or she is best equipped to contribute. Are those skills being adequately tapped? Is your competency scale tipping toward social or physical?

Don't forget that, just like at home and in your personal life, all organizations need a combination of skills and competencies. Honing your social strengths and future leaders requires that you incorporate this new capability into every aspect of your business, from product development and advertising to hiring practices and staff training. Use the online Social Quotient provided in Chapter 3 to help you better understand where you stand currently, and what you need to do to ensure your future success in this social business era. Enjoy the ride into your social future; the results are worth the effort.

3

TEST YOUR SOCIAL SKILLS

Adults are asking kids what they want to be when they grow up 'cause they're trying to get some ideas.

—Paula Poundstone

So, now that you've read the first two chapters do you think you understand what it takes to create true fans, friends, and followers and whether you have the social skills to lead the way? Or are you wondering where you and your organization fall on the social spectrum? Are you ready to discover what your specific social strengths are? Do you want to know how you compare to today's most successful leaders who have generated loyal fans and followers and increased growth?

To help you answer these questions, we've developed the Social Skills Test, an online assessment that will help you identify, with scientific certainty, how social a leader you are, where there is room for improvement, and what you can do to ensure your success. In addition, This test will evaluate your current social skills as the starting point, enabling you to grow from there.

This online-based questionnaire identifies which of the social talents or skills most accurately describe you. After you complete the test, your results—provided immediately—include a description of the three traits that you exhibited most prevalently, along with prescriptive advice on how to apply each to improve your organization's social initiatives including:

- Ways in which these traits impact how you can work with your company to make it social
- How you can ensure your company's social experience is successful with your employees and customers.

- How to recognize and overcome the weaknesses inherent in the social strengths you need to improve.

As outlined in Chapter 2, there are four primary strengths—physical, informational, emotional, and social—that come together to build an organization. However, as you will see throughout this book, your individual social talents and skills will differentiate you and your organization, if you want to participate and benefit from the emerging Social Nations that other companies and you need to build. By implementing and integrating these social traits, you will be able create and grow into a truly extraordinary organization because you will be connected on a very personal level with the people who care about you and how you do including—your fellow employees, existing customers, and potential investors. Ultimately, this assessment will help you focus on those social traits you already possess while developing new ones, all in the ongoing effort to enhance your leadership opportunities.

At Mzinga, as part of our work building and managing social nations for our clients, we have identified patterns and traits that can help you succeed. What this means is identifying the necessary people, processes and technologies you will need to inspire your customers, engage with employees and create value.

To put our qualitative insights into a more structured framework, we took what we learned from our clients and teamed up with a group of scientists to quantifiably measure individual and collective social strengths. We worked with Dr. Courtney McCashland, the founder and CEO of TalentMine, to make sense of our findings and to help us build an assessment tool that you can use to help you improve your understanding of both your strengths and weaknesses, and what you can do to strengthen the latter. Dr. McCashland is a renowned expert in identifying, measuring, and engaging individual success factors that lead to high business performance. Using proprietary questions designed to elicit natural feelings and spontaneous responses, and complex algorithms for measurement, McCashland's team developed the Social Quotient Test.

KNOW YOUR SKILLS

The beauty of the Social Quotient Test is that it tells you where and how you excel, or could naturally excel, as a social leader and manager. The test typically takes no more than 15 minutes to complete, to identify how you can most efficiently and effectively grow your social talents. Taking the test is the first step; the rest of this book provide you with the tools to start implementing your social strategies, technologies, and monitoring systems in your company.

If you are confident you already know how to apply practices that will improve your social strengths and leadership skills required in today's networked business world, you may decide not to complete the test. The choice is entirely yours. Or you may prefer to complete the assessment online and join the conversation there about "getting to social." If so, go to www.socialnationbook.com.

HOW TO GET STARTED

Before you begin to take the assessment, be aware that you may pause it, save it, and come back to it at any time—although we recommend that you take it all at one sitting. It shouldn't take long to complete—only about 15 minutes.

To get started, please go to: www .socialnationbook.com.

By clicking on this link, www.socialnationbook .com, you will reach a page marked Social Quotient Test. Follow the prompts here to begin. You will be led through a series of questions that ask you to rate how closely a situation describes you. The test will then measure your answers against the eight talent skills and report which three most closely correlate with yours.

Your results will be accompanied by suggestions on how you can leverage your strengths within your business and as a member of your team. Note that because your individual results are limited to only three traits, we have included descriptions and prescriptions for all eight in the next section. This will allow you to understand each of the social skills and consider how to acquire those you need to create a truly great organization.

Remember, you can't fail this test. You can't do better or worse than your colleague. The purpose of this test is to assess where you are in your journey to becoming a social leader as the social revolution continues to build momentum. Think of this test as just the beginning of your journey into turning your business into a social organization and yourself into a social leader. This assessment will confirm that you already have skills, and clarify which ones you can use to guide you and make you stronger as you learn, adapt, adopt, and develop new social competencies and further grow your relationships with your friends, fans, and followers.

YOUR SOCIAL QUOTIENT

Once you take the test, your results will reveal your strengths. You can use this information to further develop your skills while also identifying competencies that you or your company are lacking. No one person has every social skill or competency, and we all have our weaknesses. But this assessment can assist you by specifically identifying areas that are your strengths and areas in which you need to augment your skills with a clear plan of action for personal development.

The following eight skills or competencies are the key social characteristics that can drive connections and improve business results. Most of us excel at several of these, and as I said previously, the assessment will identify which three traits are your greatest strengths. And, as I also mentioned, we also outline all eight so that you can understand and consider how to incorporate all of them into your leadership or company.

1. Adaptor
2. Architect
3. Collaborator
4. Connector
5. Creative thinker
6. Transparent individual
7. Risk taker
8. Visionary

Adaptor

Adaptors are known for being flexible. They can easily adjust their expectations and behavior to fit dynamic situations. Adaptors are very effective at dealing with change because they can think on their feet and have the ability to look at things from a fresh perspective.

Individuals with strong adaptor skills see more than one way of doing something, and are equally comfortable with either option. They deal with situations as they happen on a real-time basis, rather than becoming rooted to one particular future outcome. Comfortable dealing with unforeseen circumstances, adaptors tend to be a calming presence in tense situations. Adaptors live in the moment and regard change as a natural occurrence. They are, therefore, good at "going with the flow."

How Adaptors Can Help an Organization Be Social

As an organization's social plans are forged, teams and priorities can shift, frequently. Adaptors can help the process stay on track by identifying where there are changes in the plan and/or how certain individuals may be impacting the project's overall success.

How Adaptors Help Sustain a Social Nation

Online communities and social networks are notoriously unpredictable. An adaptor's talents are ideally suited for recognizing behavior patterns in others that diverge from carefully laid-out plans or goals. This effort to sustain a Social Nation is most successful if you engage your constituents in the way they want to be engaged. Adaptors can evaluate how specific individuals could potentially benefit from unexpected twists and turns.

Adapters can also ferret out the problem areas. Is your organization taking big hits on Twitter? Are you having trouble drumming up enough member engagement? Adaptors can apply their skills anywhere that a change in strategy might be necessary.

A Few Words of Caution

Adaptors are often so keenly aware of the alternative approach that they sometimes look to change direction before it is necessary. Before switching things up, Adapters need to be diligent about considering whether the community will still deliver the value you're going after. First determine whether members will be able to quickly adapt to the new model, and if the cost of the change will outweigh the benefits.

Architect

Architects have a knack for seeing the big picture and drawing a blueprint for how to get where you're going. These individuals have clearly defined purpose and direction, and can see not just the destination in vivid detail, but the optimal path to it. Architects firmly believe in a mission and are confident about their ability to realize it. This confidence and depth of vision will inspire others.

How Architects Can Help an Organization Be Social

Architects see the complex path to becoming a social organization in ways others cannot. They can define this path so that others understand realistically not just the end goals but also the steps it will take to achieve them. Communicating why and how your organization's strategy path will reap the rewards and avoid the potential pitfalls is important, as is establishing short- and midterm goals, so as to sustain executive support.

How Architects Help Sustain a Social Nation

One of the most challenging aspects of maintaining a social presence is getting people to interact with to each other. Architects can help by keeping conversations going by periodically infusing them with overall vision. At the same time, allowing the crowd to influence your thinking remains important. Architects are good at rewarding positive contributions with public recognition, both personally and in an official capacity, when possible.

A Few Words of Caution

Architects have to remember that the plan is supposed to guide them to the goal, and that the goal is not to follow the plan. Architects often are so sure of their overall vision that they rigidly ignore serendipitous opportunities created by social interactions of others. Staying flexible will help an Architect deal with this, as will considering other options and paths.

Collaborator

Collaborators like to be part of a larger group; they work best when they have a support system. Collaborative individuals are genuinely interested in what others have to say, and invite open discussion to promote a common purpose. Teaming with others is natural for a Collaborator, who tends to define personal success as a function of the team's success. Collaborators are motivated by a burning need to contribute their best to the team.

How Collaborators Can Help an Organization Be Social

For an organization to become a social entity, the whole company needs to act as one community. This is where a Collaborator skills really matter, as a critical facilitator in enabling this cooperation in others. Collaborators can teach others how to interact and can set an example through their own actions. Cultivating a conscious understanding of how their efforts fit into the overall community is important to Collaborators. A Collaborator's actions can lead to greater team understanding and results.

How Collaborators Help Sustain a Social Nation

Inside the community, the pool of potential teammates has expanded to include a broad social network. Collaborators can seek out people outside the normal sphere and strike up online relationships with them. They also can be helpful in selecting a common goal and working to achieve it. Collaborators accomplish even more as community members see value coming from their own participation.

A Few Words of Caution

Collaborators are often so set on achieving consensus that they sometimes regard their own thoughts and creativity as impediments to team unity. It's important to remember that a team works best when everyone's input is considered.

Connector

Think of a connector as an orchestra conductor who brings together all of the different instruments to create a musical composition. Connectors enjoy complex situations and are skilled at moving pieces around to control the chaos. They tend to look for the perfect configuration and have no problem arranging and rearranging or devising new configurations for a better result. Connectors draw energy from enabling conversations and connections. With an orientation toward a diverse crowd, they encourage a variety of viewpoints and integrated perspectives.

How Connectors Can Help an Organization Be Social

Connectors understand who can help make social interactions vibrant and who is resisting the changes. By working with those who are stuck, identifying problems that these people can help to solve, and facilitating successes whenever possible, Connectors are integral to building a successful online community social success. Enabling those conversations through a variety of mediums helps to capture everyone's attention and engage them in discussions and actions.

How Connectors Help Sustain a Social Nation

As part of the social conversation, Connectors play several vital roles. First, they are able to become familiar with the makeup of the entire online community by identifying groups that are likely to build upon each other's ideas. Connectors can bring these groups together for lively discussions by facilitating conversations and introducing topics that are engaging to everyone involved.

Connectors are also valued members in the online community world. Members crave online social interactions and value the relationships they form there with others. Connectors can use their unique talents to identify the best potential connections. Among other things, this helps to invigorate online discussions, provides real value to end users, and improves the reputation of organizations in the marketplace.

A Few Words of Caution

Social networking is more powerful when a community is well defined as opposed to random. A Connector's intuition can sense when and where there is the potential for an authentic connection between people— even when those people may not initially recognize the potential themselves. Connectors have to take the time to inspire trust and reach an understanding of what each side might get from the other.

Creative Thinker

Creative thinkers are often first to propose new theories and ideas. They enjoy making new connections with seemingly disparate points of data, and are constantly collecting new information, while looking for novel ways to use it. People often identify Creative Thinkers as the "idea people," the inventive ones. That's because Creative Thinkers seek out innovative and unusual ways to deal with familiar challenges. They enjoy discovering new perspectives and are delighted at being enlightened.

How Creative Thinkers Can Help an Organization Be Social

As an organization becomes a part of the social revolution, Creative Thinkers will be instrumental in determining which groups of people—from employees to customers—will be most helpful and how. Creative Thinkers are skilled at finding unusual, unexpected connections among pepole and content. They can show the team how these new connections will yield business value, a critical part of any social strategy.

How Creative Thinkers Help Sustain a Social Nation

Inside any community is a wealth of new and unpredictable facts. A creative thinker is well suited to evaluating these and figuring out what unexpected value an organization can gain. To make the most of these talents, a creative thinker should have access to all sources of information (such as reports, analytics and web tracking) as well as peer perspectives before making suggestions and decisions.

A Few Words of Caution

Creative thinkers have to be careful not to get too tied up on one set of facts. If they focus all their energy on metrics, for example, they may miss out on what can be gleaned from Web tracking, releases of new content, and—most importantly—the sentiment of the community. In order to best synthesize all sources, creative thinkers need to take the time to gather statistics *and* spend time in the community.

Transparent Individual

Transparent individuals tend to be open books. They wear few social masks. You get what you see, with a transparent, open person. Their nature allows them to communicate transparently and authentically with others. And they have learned (possibly painfully) that it's worse when people find out what you've been hiding than when you share everything with them up front. As a result, transparent leaders communicate openly and accept scrutiny, positive or negative, as a natural way of life. People who are transparent tend to have an easier time gaining trust and respect from others.

How Transparency Can Help an Organization Be Social

Social media is a very open and two way based set of technologies, so it's not surprising that Transparent People see the value in this, even when others are unable to do so. They can help organizations understand why it's actually scarier to hide than it is to share. Transparency, through social networks, is here to stay, and on-line community members will go elsewhere if a business isn't enabling authentic, open conversations.

How Transparency Helps Sustain a Social Nation

Inside your on-line community, transparent individuals can make sure an organization isn't merely paying lip service to the value of transparency and openness. They can uncover information a company would benefit from sharing (such as a product road map or corporate structure) and encourage leaders to do so.

A Few Words of Caution

Transparency is great, but sometimes transparent individuals can cross the line. If this is one of your strengths, you never want to share information that has no bearing on the community. Instead of showing that you have nothing to hide, you will end up demonstrating that you are out of touch with the needs of others. Naturally transparent people have to be careful to share information with others that will excite them, not leave them snickering or perplexed. Also, they must take into account that some information, such as earnings estimates or other proprietary information may not be shared without prior approval.

Risk Taker

Risk takers have the courage to venture into unknown territory. They frequently try out novel ways of doing things, and accept that trial-and-error is an acceptable way of finding the best solution. Risk takers are motivated by making progress and reaping big rewards. They challenge the status quo and have a high tolerance for uncertainty. They know that people talk about risk a lot more than they experience it; they also know that people learn more from failing than they do from not trying.

How Risk Takers Can Help an Organizations Be Social

Risk-taking skills are critical to an organization becoming social. The risk-averse, social networking naysayer can talk all day, pointing to libel claims, copyright infringement, and worse, as justification for ignoring the social movement. But Risk Takers are willing to understand and explain the risks and rewards, rather than allowing even legitimate fears to derail a company's social networking efforts.

How Risk Takers Help Sustain a Social Nation
Risk takers should share their ideas to advance community progress. They can help by looking for others to join their cause and make their vision a reality.

A Few Words of Caution
It's important to remember that not all risks are worth taking. Risk takers have to balance the size of the reward against the risk to determine how likely success is. While a risk taker is pushing colleagues and fellow community members forward, it's essential that they simultaneously listen to them as well, since they may have valid concerns.

Visionary

A visionary is the kind of person who is energized by possibilities. Visionaries tend not to focus on obstacles, but rather on the conviction that there is a way to challenge the status quo to reach an ideal future state. Visionaries are not bound by limits and often are called upon to inspire others to imagine alternative outcomes and solutions. They are willing to invest now to build for a better future.

How Visionaries Can Help an Organization Be Social
Colleagues view visionaries as people who can identify the next big trends before they even happen. They seem to have intuitive foresight, enabling them to determine long-term, best-case scenarios for a company's social initiatives. They partner well with others, especially those who excel in creating detailed plans, to build a long-range social strategy.

How Visionaries Help Sustain a Social Nation

Inside a community, a Visionary's ideas may often be seen as controversial or impossible to achieve. Yet, a steady stream of controversial ideas can spur some of the best and most creative thinking. That's why Visionaries can be the catalyst for exciting on-line community building.

A Few Words of Caution

Visionaries have to be careful not to fall into the trap of believing that more pragmatic thinkers have a limited understanding. Instead, they should encourage criticism as well as praise. A dose of pragmatism will help to realize the most extraordinary of ideas.

THE JOURNEY BEGINS NOW

No matter what your personal assessment reveals about your specific social leadership skills (or lack thereof), you can be confident that you do have social skills. We all do. We're all social. How else would we succeed in our personal lives, building relationships with friends and family members?. Now all we have to do is learn to apply those social skills to work, to profit from them.

Strengths and skills are developed over time. There is no magic pill to take, book to read, or workshop to attend that will instantly transform your skills. But regardless of where you fall on this assessment, the important thing to remember is that, ultimately, you want to bridge two worlds: the work world and the personal world. This means taking skills that you already know and recognize and use in your personal life and bring them into your professional life. That's how you can make life and work and everything in between social.

What follows are the tools and prescriptions that can help you build your own social skills and communities. Part 2 of *Social Nation* focuses on what you can do to hone your skills and generate value. Now is the time to fine-tune your skills, while members of your organization and your leaders are doing the same. Welcome to the beginning of building your own Social Nation.

PART 2

SEVEN PRINCIPLES FOR BUILDING YOUR SOCIAL NATION

In the end, it is important to remember that we cannot become what we need to be by remaining what we are.

—Max De Pree

4

PRINCIPLE 1: DEVELOP YOUR SOCIAL SKILLS

My humanity is bound up in yours, for we can only be human together.
                              —Bishop Desmond Tutu

Staring into the camera, Gary Vaynerchuk is enunciating each syllable he speaks with intense precision, all the while gesturing enthusiastically with his hands. He's a bit mesmerizing to watch, what with his incredibly expressive face and the fact that he spits every so often due to his exacting pronunciation. Vaynerchuk is talking about wine. Only he's talking about it in a more passionate way than you've ever heard almost anyone talk about wine.

He's taken out the pompous nonsense and all the snootiness associated with oenophiles and is just talking like a regular guy from New Jersey, which he is, or was. Every few minutes he finds a way to make a reference to the New York Jets, his other passion, and has already told his viewers about his just-born nephew, Max.

A wine guru, with an encyclopedic knowledge of wines, Vaynerchuk, at 34, is an on online and offline sensation. He has a weekday Webcast called "The Thunder Show," which draws as many as 90,000 viewers. He also has more than 847,000 followers on Twitter and more than 36,500 fans on Facebook.

Vaynerchuk started out working in his father's liquor store when he was just a kid. He hated it. After college, he convinced his father to let him take the business online, and in 2006 he started Wine Library TV.

CONNECTING WITH PEOPLE

Vaynerchuk connects people to wine to build his own Wine Nation. He makes it accessible, understandable, and anything but intimidating. After swirling it around in his glass, but before tasting the wine, Gary always goes for a "sniffy sniff," as he likes to say. He doesn't talk about wine the way wine magazines write about wine. He talks about it so that regular people can understand it. "Kiwi with white pepper," "grassy," "mossy," "dirt," and "pastry cream" are words he uses to describe whites he tastes one particular day. He swishes his wine with gusto then spits into his metal Jets bucket.

To build his Social Nation, Vaynerchuk has personalized wine and the sale of wine. He engages viewers and other social media users, and closes out every Webcam episode by posing a question to his audience: "What's a white you're drinking now?" he asks. He encourages viewers to do more than just post the name of a wine. He wants people to share their own stories, explain where they first tasted the wine, what it smells like, and how it feels on their tongue.

"I share so much," he says. "I want to interact. I want to have conversations." Sometimes, he even calls this "conversating." Every day Vaynerchuk encourages his viewers to talk to each other—adding that it's perfectly acceptable if they want to talk something other than wine. He just wants to connect with his audience. He's made wine personal, and it keeps people coming back. Vaynerchuk says the whole reason for doing this show is to get people "to try new things." And try they do. Wine makers have reported spikes in sales when he mentions their products.

Open,Transparent, Social Leadership

Gary Vee—Vaynerchuk's nickname for himself—is known for being brash, and could easily be misunderstood as a self-centered egotist, but all you have to do is dig down a little further to see that he's motivated by his audience, and puts them first. He cares about what they want and need, not what he has decided they need and want. The Jim Cramer of wine, he initially appears to be a wild and opinionated one-man act.

Yet Vaynerchuk doesn't think of himself quite that way. After all, he's interacting with friends, fans and followers. He's communicating with his audience while simultaneously encouraging them to talk to each other. He's putting people at ease about a beverage and a subject that has long been out of reach for many. Vaynerchuk laughs at himself and he listens to what viewers, readers, and customers say. Ultimately, he tends to the wants and needs of his audience to drive results.

Vaynerchuk is known for returning every email he receives, and some days he receives as many as 1,000. He doesn't always do it within 24 hours, but he does it, because he knows that people want to be acknowledged and heard. Vaynerchuk appreciates the people who support him and his business—his community. If they're willing to buy wine from him, he's willing to do something to make them feel like they are special—members of his inner, social circle. Vaynerchuk actually sees his business as a series of personal relationships, rather than one based solely on the sale of wine (either online or in the store).

Consequently, he tries to make every interaction memorable and satisfying for his customers. He demonstrates his belief in this by living it. One December, three days before Christmas, Vaynerchuk heard that a woman had called his company to complain that her case of white zinfandel hadn't yet arrived. Vaynerchuk knew the bottles would never get to her house in time for the holiday, so he loaded a case into his car and drove three hours to Westchester, New York, to hand-deliver the wine.

Do What Works for You to Build Committed Fans and Followers

Gary Vaynerchuk has created an impressive social brand and network for himself and his business. He has mastered the skill of social leadership which has made him wildly successful. His one-man, personality-driven, wine shows aren't the style of most leaders today—it's not how they lead or think about their businesses. That's okay, because, as Vaynerchuk says, it isn't for everyone. You can only be successful if you're doing what is authentic to you.

For Vaynerchuk, authentic open communications means running a low-budget, highly opinionated online show, in tandem with a highly successful retail wine operation. For him, this works because he's combined those entities with a well-established social network that follows him online and offline through his shtick. In today's increasingly social world, leaders will need to stand out from the crowd and connect with their fans on a personal and social basis.

Vaynerchuk strives to create something personal with each and every customer or audience member he touches. "Making connections, creating, and continuing meaningful interactions with other people, whether in person or in the digital domain, is the only reason we're here," he writes. If that's what drives *you* in a truly authentic way, then followship will work for you, your audience and your customers. Vaynerchuk also demonstrates that he knows how to use social media without neglecting the personal, one-to-one interactions that also matter to people. He understands that individual followers and supporters want attention and need to feel connected, and that they are satisfied when they have made a personal connection.

A SOCIAL NATION FOR WOMEN

Being a social leader and developing the open management skills that Gary Vaynerchuk has doesn't mean you have to have tens of thousands of Twitter followers or be a fanatic Facebooker, but it does mean living by today's increasingly social principles. It means developing your social skills so you can help your company build friends, fans, and followers that can help you benefit the way Vaynerchuk benefits from wines sales.

Take Andrea Jung. When she was named CEO of Avon, her challenge was to turn the 123-year-old cosmetics company into something more

than a stodgy brand that many people equated with grandma's makeup. She was charged with making the brand social, recognizable, and something women wanted to connect with. Since 2001, she has done just that, through both social and personal ways, and now Avon is known worldwide as "the company for women."

To help change the company's outdated image, Jung established partnerships with Hollywood stars and singers, most notably Reese Witherspoon, while continuing to rely on "Avon Ladies" to promote and sell the company's products. It's a social model, by which the women are empowered to engage and sell to other women. They talk, share, and show others why they believe these are great products, priced right, that fit women's needs.

Many of the Avon ladies make as much as $800 a month working just part-time; others take it on as a full-time job and earn much more. Either way, the company's saleswomen are empowered to make money on behalf of Avon; and they have a vested interest in the customer being happy and the company being successful. Jung supports the individual saleswomen, and talks regularly about how being an Avon Lady requires that you make connections with people who trust you while talking with them about what matters to both of you.

Social Leadership Means Growth, Even During Recessions

With more than 6 million independent contractors (true followers, not just Twitterers or Facebook fans) around the world, Avon was one of few companies able to chart growth during the recession of 2008 and 2009. Part of the reason is that Jung is in touch with the women everywhere, from the sidewalks to the corner offices. on a personal level. When the economy slumped, she pulled together her management team and asked Avon to capitalize on what it had to offer to women—less-expensive, high-quality products (on the product side) and empowerment through part-time sales jobs (on the people side).

There were many women looking to make some extra cash or pick up a part-time job, so Jung launched a campaign to recruit them as Avon Ladies. Whereas big purchases—such as houses, cars, and vacations—tend to be put on hold during recessions, women don't usually cut back on cosmetics. Seen as a necessity by some and an allowable indulgence by others (they're much cheaper than a trip to Europe, after all), Jung was confident women would keep buying Avon. They did. In 2009, shares rose 49 percent.

In January 2008, Jung joined the Apple Inc. board, and director Millard Drexler, CEO of J. Crew Group Inc., said, "She didn't come on the board telling others what to do. She was low-key, humble; listening more than she spoke." That's social.

For a woman who has an $11 million salary and has been named to many of the lists that rank powerful and influential leaders, Jung stays closely connected to her core values. She relies on something her father told her years ago. "It's nice to be important, but it's far more important to be nice." It's that caring, compassionate, thoughtful attitude that's at the heart of being a social leader.

LEADING SOCIALLY CAN HELP YOU GET AND STAY AHEAD

Leading socially and designing your business as a social organization that connects personally and emotionally with your communities of employees and customers is challenging. However, every one of us is born with natural social skills, although many of us reserve these skills for the times we are with family or friends. It's time for everyone to bring social sensibilities to work and understand their place in business.

Studies show that women have an easier time than men bringing these social skills to work. Women leaders tend to exhibit more social and emotional skills—sharing, caring, and putting others first. According to a 2008 issue of the *McKinsey Quarterly*, women tend to make deeper emotional connections with colleagues and business partners.[1]

Many of today's most successful CEOs are beginning to integrate less traditional leadership skills into their business processes and strategies.

---

[1]Joanna Barsh, Susie Cranston, and Rebecca Craske, "Centered Leadership: How Talented Women Thrive," *McKinsey Quarterly*, 2008, N4.

The business world and board rooms are beginning to benefit on a more regular basis from people who are comfortable tapping into their passions with interconnectedness, the idea of putting others' needs first, and finding motivation in helping others succeed. These are the leadership skills that both Andrea Jung and Gary Vaynerchuk have been relying on to propel themselves and their businesses forward.

FINDING THE NEW SOCIAL LEADERS IN YOUR ORGANIZATION TO CREATE CHANGE

Former eBay CEO Meg Whitman had a unique view on being a social leader. In 2001, as she was building eBay's leadership team, she struggled to find the right people to help her scale her company because of the traditional prejudices she found in many of the men and women she interviewed. The candidates for management positions Whitman encountered were more interested in controlling the eBay community than they were in facilitating it; they were too uncomfortable allowing the user community to define what workcd for them and what did not.

Whitman, who was an early adopter of the social leadership

concept, understood the power of building a nation for like-minded people who wanted to buy and sell their own personal overstock. She also saw the value in turning over much of the control to the crowd and wasn't threatened by this. Instead, she saw potential and opportunity. Her business model was built on empowering others to decide what they wanted to sell, how they wanted to sell it, and the rewards (financial and otherwise) that would follow. Whitman saw it as eBay's role to facilitate those interactions, not control them.

EBay continues to rely on socially enabled business models, which have allowed for its continued growth and profitability. The company's success also serves as an example for other ventures such as etsy.com, an online crafts fair of sorts, through which vendors and artists can sell handmade goods. EBay and Etsy have successfully created communities of buyers and sellers through an open marketplace.

SOCIAL LEADERS PUT OTHERS FIRST

Why should you add followship skills to your traditional leadership skills? Vast and highly connected socially networked communities of employees, partners, customers, and others can help drive your business to new heights. This happens when you allow and enable those people to help create new products, generate marketing messages that are compelling, hire people who care and are connected, and build communities of current and prospective customers who want to buy your products.

To do all of this successfully, you need to think about your community first, and understand their individual wants and needs. Social leaders understand this; they also understand the importance of starting with their communities, rather than with their products and services. Gary Vaynerchuk, for example, is more interested in talking with his community about wine, and less concerned about where its members go to buy it. And at Avon, the primary focus is on the women who are selling the products and the women who are buying them. The products, which unquestionably have to be extraordinary, come next.

A social leader's most valuable skills are rooted in building and managing communities for the benefit of his or her business, which should ultimately be a community unto itself, rather than merely a product or a service. You can control the type of leader you are, whether as the CEO or department head. You have the power to change your leadership, adapt your style, and become social.

Being a social leader doesn't just mean connecting people, facilitating their interactions, and using today's technologies to help others succeed, however. Rather, social leadership also involves creating valuable businesses that benefit from harnessing people's emotions, connections, and relationships so that they offer more than just great products and services in today's commodities-crowded world. Being a social leader now requires you to make strong emotional and social connections with networks of customers and employees who can help you go from good to great and from great to extraordinary.

PRESCRIPTIONS FOR YOUR SOCIAL SKILLS

Building your social leadership skills is something you and only you can do. This is about you accepting that you need to make changes in your core skills and competencies, to improve your own social skills and your company's social strengths. This is the first step. Developing and then improving on your social skills as a social leader, so that your business can achieves its true potential, starts with the following seven prescriptions.

1. Get to Know the People around You

Care about the people who work for you. Get to know them, understand what motivates them, what inspires them, and what they want when they come to work. Andrea Jung inherited a company that was founded on the business model of empowering women economically. When she talks about focusing on others, she points out that the entire Avon model is built around women who work for themselves, not for the CEO.

To focus on others also means listening to the desires of and complaints from the people in your network. Remembering names matters. Find out what matters to the individuals and communities around you so that you can engage with them and provide for them, on their terms.

At Avon, Jung has worked hard to create an environment that is sensitive to family needs. Employees are, for example, allowed to leave work in order to attend their kids' recitals or sports events. That's what matters to her employees. Be sure to deliver on what your partners and employees want. In the end, they will reward you with their time and loyalty (as employees) and money (as customers). Finally, seek out their feedback to make sure that you are constantly in touch with what your employees and customers want. It changes constantly.

2. Know What You Are Not

Honestly and accurately assess who you are, what type of leader you are, which skills you possess and which ones you lack. Commit to improving your weakest strengths and developing your social and emotional skill sets. It's especially important in today's social world, or while building your own Social Nation, to recognize your weaknesses and surround yourself or your business with professionals who compliment you and your skills. Don't hire 10 more people just like you. Hire those who are nothing like you and can bring new skills and competencies to the table. Look at your company, your teams, and your board.

3. Let Others Lead, While You Follow

Traditional leadership no longer works in the social business world. Subjugate your own needs for the betterment of the community. Follow your leadership team, listen to your newest hires, put yourself where they are, and hear the other perspectives. Imagine you are looking at the world from their position, not yours. Hand over the reins and let your employees lead the way. This means giving them permission to succeed as well as fail, with you being supportive in the background and understanding that you are not in control and cannot always be in control.

Allow the group, the collective, to drive the agenda while recognizing that the health of the community requires that the community form itself, not that you dictate what it looks like. Social leaders set context, not content. Don't get me wrong: I am not suggesting that you let your company run wild. What I am saying is that, instead, establish parameters then step back to see what happens—creatively, socially, and financially—within that context.

4. Know How Others Perceive You

Are you intimidating? Do you have a loud and booming voice that dominates any room you walk into? For a change, be silent; sit back from the table, or in the corner of the room; minimize your presence and pay attention to how your dynamic changes the tenor of a conversation or meeting. It's difficult to know how you actually come across, even when you have every intention of being sensitive to those around you. Even leaders who desperately want to get it right, and do care, have a hard time knowing how others perceive them.

As someone who is tall and has a booming voice, I know that I can be intimidating to the people around me. I don't mean to be, and I work hard to be sensitive to this, but I find I still have to take extra measures to allow others to feel comfortable around me. To that end, I sit back from tables, rather than looming over them; I focus actively on speaking in a quieter voice—or I don't talk at all. And I rely on people I trust to tell me when I'm coming across too strong.

5. Embrace a Social Culture

Social culture is built by telling people that they *own* their actions, through transparency. A social organization embodies an openness of expression, an openness of networks, and an openness that allows for both risks and rewards. Social culture stands for something that only your company can create. It's something personal that comes from within. That's what makes it lasting, exciting, powerful, and magnetic.

Principle 2 in the next chapter looks in detail at how to build a social culture. But before it can be built, leadership has to embrace it, and support it. In a social business, culture is the glue that holds the entire operation together, so that when you aren't there the ship runs without you. Culture enables everything to happen, even without you. When you are on vacation, in a board meeting, or at a conference, your operation hums and your employees aren't looking around for their leader to tell them what to do.

6. Focus on What's in It for Others

Traditional business leaders think about the products they build, the services they offer, and the returns they can expect before they think about anything else. Social leaders start by thinking about what's in it for other people as they begin to build a loyal following. If you do the same, your outcomes will be better aligned with your audience, and your returns will be greater.

A traditional model starts with the business in mind, the product you're going to sell, and the people you'll hire to make it happen. Social leaders focus on other people first and determine how the business can best meet *their* needs. Gary Vaynerchuk meets the needs of his customers by providing information and making wine accessible and easy to understand.

Social models are revenue models that allow others to benefit from what you are offering while connecting emotively. This means aligning the interests of your customers and employees with those of your business. Show them what's in it for them. The more you do, the more they will benefit; and the more they benefit, the more they will return to you.

7. Remember, Business *Is* Personal

Like it or not people are bringing themselves, their personalities, their voices and their personal selves to work. Social leaders embrace this because they understand that it enhances business. By bringing the personal to work, social leaders can demonstrate humility, caring, and openness. By talking to people at work the way you would talk to people at home or at your kid's soccer game, you will encourage them to talk.

Making business personal is about demonstrating that you aren't just a leader, but that you're a person, too, with passions, interests, fears, and family and friends. Listening to what people want, how they feel, and what makes them tick enables social businesses to improve customer experiences and create attractive communities. Make your business social and bring your version of personal to work. You don't have to divulge family secrets; just show people that you're human.

Becoming a social leader and maintaining social leadership skills can be challenging, as I said earlier. It may require you to push yourself to new limits. And like any sport or skill or relationship, it takes practice. No amount of practice will make you perfect, of course, but you can get pretty close. And the more you practice, the easier it will become. The closer you get to mastering social skills, the more rewards—professionally, personally, and financially—you will discover. There is no finite end. This is a practice, a journey. It doesn't end, but it does get easier, more enjoyable, and more rewarding the farther along you go.

In a December 10, 2009, post on ''Seth Godin's Blog'' Godin wrote a piece titled ''The reason social media is so difficult for most organizations.'' Godin wrote, ''It's

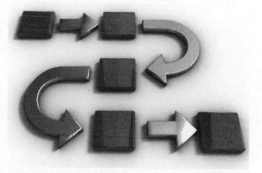

a process, not an event. Dating is a process. So is losing weight, being a public company, and building a brand. On the other hand, putting up a trade show booth is an event. So are going public and having surgery. Events are easier to manage, pay for, and get excited about. Processes build results for the long haul.''

Building your Social Leadership skills is a journey and one that you will need to embrace if you want to build a Social Nation. Becoming a social leader—whether a team leader, manager, or individual contributor—means evolving into someone who is open and authentic, and who remembers to practice followship (our view of social leadership) every day. The process will become more and more intuitive, even if it doesn't start out that way. The more you practice followship, the more you will experience it, the easier it will become, and the more rewards it will bring.

5

PRINCIPLE 2: LET CULTURE LEAD THE WAY

When shall we learn that we are all related one to the other, that we are all members of one body?

—Helen Keller

When Tony Hsieh joined Zappos in 1999 as co-CEO he had two goals: to reach $1 billion in sales within 10 years, and to make *Fortune* magazine's list of 100 Best Companies to Work For. The first he did by the end of 2008; a year later, he made the coveted list when the online shoe retailer debuted at No. 23.

Zappos has long been known for its customer-service-centered culture—free shipping and return shipping being the hallmarks—and call center operators who are willing to spend hours, literally, on the phone to give customers a good, personal experience. Hsieh has built a Service Nation. That said, he insists culture is even more important; he knows that without it he would have never achieved his original goals.

Hsieh says the Zappos culture (and the value that was created from it) is built on the company's 10 core values, which are known by every employee, repeated often, and emblazoned on signs around the company's Henderson, Nevada, headquarters. The Zappos values are listed here, in bold; and though most are self-explanatory, we've summarized their objectives.

1. *Deliver WOW Through Service:* Go above and beyond, while doing things in unconventional, unexpected ways so as to leave people with "a positive story they can take with them the rest of their lives."
2. *Embrace and Drive Change:* Always be looking for ways to change things for the better; otherwise, improvements will never happen.

3. *Create Fun and a Little Weirdness:* Hsieh supports wacky, odd personalities and happenings, while fostering creative work and spirits.
4. *Be Adventurous, Creative, and Open-Minded:* Take risks, make mistakes, and go with your "gut feeling," something the company openly supports.
5. *Pursue Growth and Learning:* Zappos encourages personal and professional growth, which also means tackling problems head-on while always trying to improve.
6. *Build Open and Honest Relationships with Communication:* Act with strength and integrity, and always be aware of how you're making someone else feel.
7. *Build a Positive Team and Family Spirit:* The best decisions come from the bottom up, which means watching out for everyone and encouraging coworkers, especially the ones you supervise. Spending time together outside work helps forge bonds within the office.
8. *Do More with Less:* Improve efficiency and operations, with fewer resources and complications.
9. *Be Passionate and Determined:* Be passionate about the culture and the business, and remain positive, because it inspires others.
10. *Be Humble:* Celebrate personal, team, and company wins, but in a respectful way. Zappos calls it "quiet confidence."

Hsieh understands that building his company around these core principles produces true value. Further, he recognizes the importance of converting employees into active fans and followers of the company he is trying to build. As part of that philosophy, each year Hsieh asks every employee to contribute short, personal essays on these core values, which are then compiled into an unedited book that is distributed to all Zappos employees.

Hsieh believes it's essential to start with core values when building a business. He says those core values need to resonate with the people who make up your organization (employees), so that if you, as CEO, disappear, the values endure; they serve as the glue that holds your employee community together. "The analogy I would use is that if you think of employees as, say, plants, I don't see myself as the tallest plant that everyone aspires to be. I see my role as being the architect of the greenhouses, and they'll figure out how to grow on their own," explains Hsieh.

COMPARE ZAPPOS TO GENERAL MOTORS . . . YOU GET THE POINT

Now compare the core values of General Motors to those of Zappos. The contrast is startling. Zappos built Service Nation in less than a decade and yet General Motors failed to build and sustain Driver's Nation over a century in no small part because of a lack of social culture and understanding. GM's culture statement is buried at the bottom of one of the pages on the company's website about corporate social responsibility. It's rather boring and uninspiring.

> GM's vision is to be the world leader in transportation products and related services. We will earn our customers' enthusiasm through continuous improvement driven by the integrity, teamwork, and innovation of GM people. Becoming the best is an unending journey, a constantly changing destination. But that's where we're determined to drive—one car, one truck, one customer at a time.
>
> We have defined six core values to guide our global business conduct:
>
> - Customer enthusiasm
> - Integrity
> - Teamwork
> - Innovation
> - Continuous improvement
> - Individual respect and responsibility
>
> Our employees conduct their day-to-day business with the strong foundation of our core values.

Don't Be Boring, Be Emotive If You Want to Connect

In reviewing GM's statement, it's clear that there is nothing egregiously "wrong" in it; but it is impersonal and it's certainly not emotive or social. It is apparent the company just doesn't get the importance of connecting, on a personal or social level with their constituents. Words matter, but putting them into effect is even more important, as witnessed by both Zappos and GM.

Before joining Zappos, Hsieh says he experienced firsthand what it was like to work in a negative, uninspiring, and impersonal business culture. He was determined to never subject anyone to that. He vowed to create a culture that was infectious and exciting, personal and engaging, social and connected. "Businesses often forget about the culture, and ultimately, they suffer for it because you can't deliver good service from unhappy employees," he said in a *Footwear News* article, May 4, 2009. More importantly, there is no chance of building Social Nation if you're not inspiring, connecting and communicating with those around you.

Where Culture Starts, Business Results Follow

At Zappos, creating value starts with culture. And that culture starts with how people are hired, which is the first step in creating fans and Zappos fanatics. Potential hires go through two rounds of interviews. The first is the "culture interview" in which potential candidates are asked questions such as, "How weird are you, on a scale of 1 of 10?" Hsieh says the best fit for the company is someone who falls around a 7 or 8. Another question is: "What is your theme song?"

Although unconventional, these queries are meant to weed out the people who just won't fit in, either because they are too straitlaced, too wacky, or too arrogant. Hsieh's intent is to really get to know what makes each individual an individual. In other words, he makes hiring personal.

New hires at Zappos must complete four weeks of training. The first two are classroom-based and the next two are held in the call center. Then comes the now-famous offer of $2,000 *to quit* (that's right, *paid to quit*). This quitting bonus started in 2005 when Hsieh began offering trainees $100 to jump ship. Over the years he says it has helped to motivate the bad seeds to move on, so Hsieh is happy to give people an incentive to leave. For those who truly want to be there, $2,000 won't be tempting. In fact, very few people take it.

Once in, new employees find the company to be extremely personal and social; always focused on building community, yet full of fun and oddball gimmicks, such as costume parades around the office and a Dance Dance Revolution machine in the lobby. Free popcorn and free meals are provided; and employees are encouraged to use social media to communicate with each other and the outside world (customers, prospects, partners). Hsieh has no qualms about revealing to customers and employees alike what's being said, even if it isn't always positive, because he understands that "personal sells." He understands that to be successful he needs to let culture lead the way—both personally and organizationally.

Trusting Others to Help You Succeed

There are more serious aspects of Hsieh's culture, too. More important than the fun atmosphere at work is that he empowers his employees and embraces them as individuals, whom he trusts to act on their own good judgment. He treats them as trusted family members. Call-center reps are free to decide when someone should be awarded a complimentary pair of shoes, or be refunded on defective ones. All reps are asked to send about a dozen personal notes to customers each day, and everyone is encouraged to be guided by a "personal emotional connection" with callers.

The company demonstrates that there is a culture of personal and social trust by allowing these call-center operators to make decisions without having to always check with a supervisor. Operators have no script, and their calls aren't timed. This encourages them to take the time to make a human connection with the person on the other end of the line. They talk to people like people, not robots. It's social. Zappos employees have even been known to send flowers to customers. One bouquet went to a widow who had just recently lost her husband; she had called to return a pair of boots she had purchased for him just before he died.

Hsieh has found a way to turn ordering shoes into an opportunity for people to connect authentically with one another on a very personal level, to build a loyal following of fans that drive his business.

Bringing Bits of Life to Work

An avid reader, Hsieh also started a library for all employees and visitors to use, as a way to encourage others to dive into books. Because the company's core values include personal and professional growth, books on culture, business, and self-help are available for the taking. It's also worth mentioning that Hsieh doesn't have an office. He works in a cubicle, like everyone else. There's also a nap room on site; and a full-time life coach is on staff, available to counsel employees out of a slump, provide advice, or help coworkers through a difficult situation. Visiting the life coach's office does, however, mean that you must sit on the red velvet throne; no traditional chairs are provided.

Managers at Zappos are encouraged to spend 10 to 20 percent of their time with team members outside the office. Simply put, they are asked to be social with them. Hsieh says you can't feel good about where you work if you don't have a good culture. "If you get the culture right, then most of the other stuff follows."

CULTURE: MAKE IT SOCIAL, MAKE IT PERSONAL

In today's world, a truly great and valuable business like Zappos can't exist without a social and highly connected culture, one that is developed and driven by *you*. Culture defines you. It tells your customers who you are and what you stand for. It tells your employees what to expect. It starts with written and verbal communication and is given its personality, flair, and details by your actions. It's another element of building your own social skills and social success. Furthermore, if you play an active role in developing your teams and your company's culture, then you have the chance to make your company more social and, ultimately, more valuable.

A social culture provides guidelines that are based on what we all know works in our personal lives. Your culture doesn't have to appeal to everyone—just as it wouldn't for everyone in your local community. Its purpose is to create cohesion within a company or team, and this is becoming increasingly important as the people joining companies become more diverse.

Creating culture can be difficult, even harder than producing products or services. In fact, as Hsieh points out, one culture won't work for everyone. That's certainly true at Zappos; but Hsieh is okay with that. In fact, he wants to find that out sooner rather than later. Creating a social culture that helps define the company—including who you hire, what your communicate, and how you service your customers—means finding a match between your company's current personality and the current and future demands of your community members as they join the Social Nation and expect to have a voice in your organization.

If you are confident in the culture that you are building, the rest will follow. That's why, in today's social business world, it's important that culture be personal, so that individuals can relate to their work the way they relate to family when they are at home. Culture brings together family, friends, and colleagues, in order to help everyone get along better and build a community, whether at home or at work. The same is true for your customers and investors. To retain them, you need to really know them and care about them on an individual basis and build a culture that ensures that caring becomes pervasive throughout everything you do.

CULTURE IS WHAT THE OUTSIDE WORLD SEES, TOO

Starting your culture with personal values (rather than personality) will help you energize your customers, partners and employees. Culture is what you can fall back on, and rely on, and build from, because these will be motivating factors. Culture matters to the people working at your company, but it also matters to your investors, who increasingly understand that culture is the company's DNA. If the DNA is healthy, the company is healthy. If it is not, the company (just like your family) will falter, and eventually fail. In our personal lives, this means getting divorced, finding a new spouse, finding a new job, and/or relocating to a new town. In business, it means your customers will leave in pursuit of a competitor that will care more about them and better meet their needs.

Consumers can sense when your culture is a social, personal, and healthy one. Not only do customers want to purchase outstanding products and services, they really want to do business with people who provide a communal experience of belonging.

Customers want more than transactions. They want connections. Likewise, they want to connect on a personal and social level to other customers who also are purchasing your products or services. This way they can share their passions, concerns, and thoughts. After all, they are spending their hard-earned time and money on your company, so they want to talk about it.

With that in mind, let's look now at the prescriptions for creating a personal and social culture at work that will lead to actual, lasting value.

PRESCRIPTIONS FOR CREATING YOUR OWN SOCIAL CULTURE
1. Start with Core Values

While certain themes will be universal across the business world, each company will have its own unique group of people who bring with them their own unique sets of values. Listed here are the core business values by which I live and Mzinga operates. We have used them to build our company, in much the same way I have used them to build my family— to create a positive and clear sense of belonging, of commitment and direction. The most important part is that we, like others, refine them to increasingly reflect the values of our "family," so that each and every person can connect with them as individuals.

- *Take risks to break away from the rest.* It is important to fail, because if you don't take risks and fail (whether at home or in business), you won't be able to accomplish the extraordinary. In order to be the best, you have to focus on one thing, which will allow you to work on doing that one thing extremely well.
- *Create memorable interactions.* People remember the bad experiences they have more than they do the good ones. It is important to me that our people have positive community and customer interactions so that everyone is left with something memorable to remembers us.
- *Make everything easy, fun, and engaging.* Life is hard; so is business. Consequently, we want to deliver products and services that are fun and engaging and easy to use. Very few companies deliver products that connect with you personally or emotionally, and even fewer build the sort of cult

following generated by Apple. All of which means there are many opportunities in every business, including yours, to focus on making products interactive, social, and part of a following or community.

- *Put others first and the rest will follow.* We all understand this value from our personal lives. If you focus on your loved ones, and meet their needs, good things will happen. If you start with your needs, and focus primarily on your needs, good things probably won't happen. It works the same way in business. In 2007, the American Association of Retired Persons (AARP) ran a contest through YouTube called U@50, which encouraged anyone between the ages 18 and 30 to submit a brief video on what they expect their lives to be like at 50. AARP was already focused on figuring out how to meet the needs of their future 50-year-olds while demonstrating that they weren't going to rely only on current constituents to shape future communities.
- *Relinquish control to obtain what you want.* As individuals, we each want to accomplish something each day that will make us proud. Consequently, it is increasingly important that businesses relinquish control to their employees and customers so that individual desires and goals can be achieved. Allowing others to reach fulfillment while taking part in helping you achieve your goal will inspire loyalty and mutual appreciation.
- *Share the rewards with others.* Rewards can be financial or emotional. They can be based on money or self-actualization; the latter, in particular, is common in social companies. People want

to feel good about what they're doing, and be recognized for it. If companies focus on helping others gets there, they too will achieve their goals.

* *Combine excellences.* Extraordinary companies combine excellent products and services with social, personal connections. This combination is what creates a following, because being social is what matters to people today. What makes Zappos different from its competitors is that its customers (who merely buy shoes) actually matter. If you want your business to stand out from the millions of other businesses out there, you have to be different. You have to be social.

2. Ask People What They Want

A truly social culture is one that is built by listening to and embracing employee and customer desires, but it also needs to be anchored on what you think will truly differentiate your team and organization. In order to do this successfully, leaders and managers need to understand their personal and community behaviors. Companies have to understand what employees and customers want individually, as well as socially, as a community. Making your work environment social allows employees to interact with each other and organize themselves, to create a connection and commitment, which deepens ties to the company and to other individuals.

A social company should provide the framework upon which everyone—including the most outgoing as well as the most introverted—can become engaged, both online and offline. People will begin to organize organically around what they feel is most important to them as individuals. A social culture is self-sustaining; it continuously engages employees to contribute, learn from each other, and interact within the whole community.

Google Sets the Pace

At Google, work is life and life is work. Google is known for this. The company offers an abundance of employee interest groups, free meals, and weekly Friday meetings with the CEO, all of which connect people emotional and socially. Google makes sure that its employees feel great about going to work.

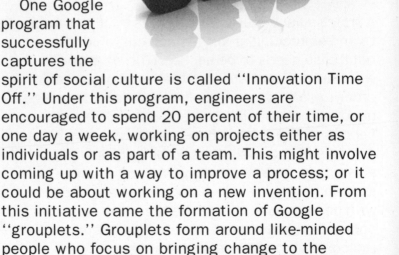

One Google program that successfully captures the spirit of social culture is called "Innovation Time Off." Under this program, engineers are encouraged to spend 20 percent of their time, or one day a week, working on projects either as individuals or as part of a team. This might involve coming up with a way to improve a process; or it could be about working on a new invention. From this initiative came the formation of Google "grouplets." Grouplets form around like-minded people who focus on bringing change to the organization. Bharat Mediratta, a Google engineer, talked about his experience building a grouplet:

> *In my 20 percent time, I started the Testing grouplet. This was born of the idea—not mine—*

*that if developers wrote automated tests as they
wrote their code, their code would be better for
it. Less time fixing bugs means more time
building stuff. We started with engineers from all
over the company meeting every couple of
weeks to brainstorm. Slowly, over time, we
started turning into activists, planning to
actually start improving things. We started
building better tools and giving informal talks to
different technical groups. We started building a
curriculum for our Nooglers—newly hired Google
employees—so that they would start off right.
With our pooled 20 percent time, we slowly
turned the organization on its axis and made
developer testing a common part of the
development practice.*

"The Google Way: Give Engineers Room,"
New York Times,
October 21, 2007

This illustrates how a company can foster a
social culture that encourages a sense of belonging,
the same way we do this with friends and family.
This display of passion and commitment is what
differentiates a social company from a good—or
even great—company. A social company is one
that connects and is personal at the most
fundamental level.

In order to be able to offer truly social rewards and
incentives, a company must be in synch with its
people and their emotive and social requirements.
You have to know what they want, what would make
them happy, before you can try to offer that up. And
the only way to get there is to listen, and then be
willing to act on what you've heard.

Bringing Laundry to Work

At Analytical Graphics, Inc. employees are welcome to bring their laundry to work. This came about because younger workers had been complaining that they didn't have time to wash their clothes. As odd as this practice sounds, chief executive Paul Graziani was open to hearing what his employees wanted when it came to company perks and culture.

That's why several years ago he also started offering free snacks, and then the occasional catered meal to his employees. The lunch options had been so slim around this Exton, Pennsylvania, company that the firm decided to bring in a full-time catering staff. Now, all employees are provided breakfast, lunch, and dinner, if they want it. Families are welcome to stop by for meals, as well, and employees may take dinner home at the end of the day. And during lunch on Fridays, the company hosts "story time," which is really an opportunity for employees to share what they are working on, further bridging a connection between departments while starting conversations among coworkers.

3. Embrace Social Technology

With more people working remotely, some even on the other side of the world from one another, it has become essential to personalize our communications with each other. By engaging your employees, listening to what they are saying, and encouraging a diversity of opinions and interests, you enable better relationships. Basic business etiquette (outlined in more detail in the next chapter) goes a long way toward helping achieve a social culture.

When connecting with your employees or investors, consider the following four Es as a guide:

- *ENGAGE* employees in active dialogue, and then *listen* to them.
- *ENCOURAGE* employee diversity, interests, and passions.
- *ENABLE* better, more meaningful relationships and actions.
- *ETIQUETTE* facilitates the best possible engagement.

4. Create a New Breed of Social Leaders

Leadership and management are still necessary within a collaborative culture; it's just less dictatorial than under traditional models. A collaborative culture embraces the free voicing and sharing of ideas, but at the end of the day, leaders and managers still need to assess and analyze those ideas, and make the final decisions. In this way, social leaders become facilitators. They still need to enable the capture and exchange of other people's ideas.

5. Celebrate Diversity and Openess

To foster a collaborative culture, you have to be open to the fact that people are going to think, act and behave differently than you do. It's important to embrace diversity, as in diversity of thought, perspective, and ways to solve problems. By doing so, you enable the entire culture, collectively, to think out of the box, and you ensure that community members feel supported and comfortable expressing their opinions and introducing their ideas, without fear of rejection or job security.

Embracing diversity means welcoming different communication styles, as well. Not everyone will be overtly communicative in a social, collaborative culture, but that doesn't mean they aren't engaged. In order for relationships and communication to be effective, you need both talkers and listeners. Some will be active participants, driving the conversations and new ideas on a daily basis. Others might contribute only when they have something substantive to share, or will share only on those topics on which they have expertise. Still others will be more reactive and responsive to the ideas of others. All of these communication styles have a place in a collaborative culture. People have different voices, and they also have different styles. Social leaders make room for all of them.

6. Find Your Path to Trust

Being collaborative and social means opening up, and even becoming vulnerable—vulnerable to criticism of your ideas, vulnerable to being ignored, vulnerable to showing people more of who you are than you might have in the past. Certainly, boundaries remain essential, but it's important for social leaders to express their vulnerability, to demonstrate that sharing new ideas and taking risks are crucial to establishing trust.

7. Don't Forget: Space Breeds Culture

People spend billions annually on home renovations, yet our office spaces are often unpleasant, if not downright suffocating. This seems cruel, given that many of us spend more time at work than we do at home. Space and place do matter when it comes to establishing and breeding a social culture, even if they are secondary. Companies find many different ways to implement space changes, to create social spaces that will enhance overall interactions.

Unilever recently took away 36 percent of employees' personal space after company executives realized that much of it wasn't being used. Rather, they found, people were convening in hallways, open spaces, and common areas. Therefore, the company's office was redesigned around "agile" space, which in essence is a large open area that can be reconfigured each day depending on the needs of the people using it. In essence, Unilever made its workspace a social one.

Financial services company, ING Group, has its headquarters in Amsterdam, where more than 2,500 people work in an S-shaped building with 10 towers and various walkways connecting them all. The walkways are decorated with more than $1 million in original art. There are no square or rectangular rooms, and no one sits more than 18 feet from a window. The building was purposely planned to create a certain sense of place that implies openness and energy.

Of course, not all companies can spend millions of dollars on art or renovations; the point is, creating a social space is important.

A social leader can distinguish him- or herself when it comes to having a vision and taking responsibility for the course set by his or her company. But it's crucial for the company culture that this same leader not be physically separate from the organizational body. Being present and integrated into an office space is important.

A number of companies started giving away free food, and a lot of it, to their employees during the dot-com era. Everyone loves to eat, and free food always seems to taste better. But, in the social era, it's no longer about the food, per se. Instead, serving meals is a way of encouraging people to come out of their offices, step away from their keyboards, and flow into the same space, to see one another, to interact—to, simply, come together. Coming together, finding comfortable, inspiring places to be together and connect over shared interests, goals, or ideas, is social.

In the end, letting culture lead the way means allowing your core values to become integral to every piece of your Social Nation building process. This includes defining who you hire, how you service your customers, and the goals you set, both financial and otherwise. Chapter 6, the final one about what *you* can do to create social success, is about how you do and say things while creating connections and relationships. We call this *social etiquette*.

6

PRINCIPLE 3: MIND YOUR ONLINE AND OFFLINE MANNERS

We discover ourselves through others.
—Carl Jung

How you say something—your tone, your expression, your written and verbal communications—is often more important than what you say. That has always been true at home and now it is becoming increasingly important at work as you seek to build fans, followers, and friends in every aspect of your business. In that spirit, achieving the right tone of voice is critical in creating a community of people in the social web who care about you and your organization. Having good manners, being gracious, and saying thank you all count.

YOU CAN STILL LEARN FROM EMILY POST

The arbiter of etiquette and good manners, Emily Post, spent summers in picturesque Bar Harbor, Maine, where August breezes can be refreshing, and the ocean views are, simply, stunning. Now teeming with ice cream shops and tour buses, Bar Harbor used to be a refined vacation getaway where lawn parties, carriage rides to the top of Cadillac Mountain, and yachting were daily activities.

Post always brought her German shepherd, Bruno, along for the summer. One year, a small yappy dog next door yapped at Bruno day after day—Bruno was in one yard; the yappy dog in another.

As Post's great-grandson, Peter Post, tells the story, one day the barking stopped. All was quiet outside. No yappy, annoying dog. When his great-grandmother looked outside to see why the noise had stopped, she saw Bruno holding the yappy dog in his mouth. Not sure what might happen next, Post just watched. Bruno sauntered down to a nearby dock, walked to the end of it, and promptly dumped the little dog into the water. Then he turned around and walked home. Eventually, the yappy dog did the same. From that moment on, the two got along marvelously well.

Remember Bruno's Choices

"It's not what you do; it's how you do it," says Peter Post. "Bruno solved the problem and built a relationship at the same time." In human terms, we may see Bruno as a fierce dog, but in animal terms he had two choices. He could have mauled the small dog; instead he chose to show the pest that he'd had enough and wanted the harassing barking to stop.

As a director of the Emily Post Institute, syndicated columnist and author of several books on online etiquette, Peter Post tells this story to illustrate that we all have options as we seek to create friends and fans that can help us achieve our goals. Since his great-grandmother's time, the basic rules of etiquette have changed little.

Emily Post's first book, *Etiquette* was published in July 1922. It quickly became the bible on how to be social, how to listen, share, engage in conversation, and show an interest in others. Of course, *Etiquette* also sorts out which fork we should use with which dish. But at its essence the book remains a guidepost for how to appropriately use social media to engage your customers and inspire employees.

The Emily Post Institute was founded in 1946 and is now located in Burlington, Vermont. The focus at the institute remains on differentiating between good behavior and bad, between acceptable and unacceptable ways of interacting with others. The rules still apply—to every era, from the 1920s to today's interconnected, Web 2.0 world, which we now call the Social Nation. Yet, using social media is interpreted by many as having a pass to leave manners and etiquette behind.

Netiquette (online etiquette) isn't something Emily Post had to think about. But, her great-grandson says many of the same principles she initially wrote still apply in today's online business and personal interactions. Many of these concepts of etiquette, he says, have changed little in the past century. To start, Peter Post talks about etiquette being predicated on three fundamental principles: being considerate, respectful, and honest. All three remain crucial in today's business world in order to profit in the Social Nation.

"How" Matters When Building Relationships

When explaining how to understand and implement etiquette, Post suggests focusing on two concepts. The first is this notion of *how* you do something (think of Bruno): "How will this affect the way people interact with you," he explains. The second most fundamental principle has to do with perspective. "In business, it's the perspective of the other person that matters, especially if your goal is to build friends and fans who can help you succeed.'' It's the other person's opinion that matters, not yours.

In other words, this is about putting others first. Post says that you may think you look great or sound polite or are acting respectfully, but what really matters is whether other people think you look appropriate, are being respectful, and are acting politely. If they don't, it will have a negative impact. In this case, Post says, this means you will have to change your orientation.

Just as business has to ask how it can serve other people's needs, we need to understand how others see us (both online and off), so that we can improve our chances at success. Above all else, Post says this requires listening to people. The more we listen, and the more we understand someone else's needs, the more successful we can be in today's socially connected world. The less we listen, or try to pretend we're listening (i.e., without authenticity) the more irritated and turned off other people will become.

Guidelines Are Critical in Creating Relationships

When it comes to actual guidelines, Post says, ''People like to know what to do.'' Rules or guidelines provide boundaries and help people to feel comfortable, by letting them know what is expected of them and having something to measure themselves against. It's also okay to change the rules, to adapt them to what works best for you, your business, and/or your teams. And whether you're acting as an individual or as a member of a team, you should be behaving with similar etiquette in mind. Team members will be required to collaborate and coordinate and defer to others, whereas individuals won't have to do this as often. Regardless, the *how* remains the same.

As work and life blend, and technology becomes more a part of our daily personal and professional interactions, we're bound to become confused. Post encourages people to be aware that they have to be "on" much more frequently than just when they are in the office. Tweeting about something personal, sharing information on Facebook, or sending an email that is intended for only one person, can all become public very quickly. The line between public and private is blurring, and Post says it's happening because individuals fail to remember that often what we think is private (email, our Facebook posts) is anything but.

WATCH HOW YOU SAY IT BECAUSE EVERYONE CAN SEE IT

So, how do you develop individual and collective Netiquette at your company as you seek to build high-quality relationships that go well beyond tweeting? Do you do it by writing and distributing a 40-page policy statement, or remind people over the public address system to say please and thank you? Some of the social signals are subjective, and so are hard to teach, and are especially hard to number in a to-do list.

There is still something to be said for a company providing written procedures or manuals that can be used to help guide its teams and individuals in building a community that is vested in the firm's success. Written rules help you to establish guidelines that provide staff with an understanding of what is expected of them. And in today's litigious world, such rules and regulations have become increasingly helpful to businesses—if not a legal necessity. Establishing some ground rules makes it a lot easier to "play the game," change the rules when necessary, and get creative within the framework. Leaving expectations open to interpretation and assuming people will understand what is required of them isn't beneficial, productive, or helpful.

Post isn't kidding when he says it's important to train employees in business etiquette. Many of them come out of college, are used to being the center of attention, and often get what they want when they want it. They feel and act entitled and aren't used to having to work hard to succeed. When they enter the work world (your company), it's quite a shock.

Embracing Good Etiquette in Business Matters

Post suggests that to build your own successful Social Nation, companies have to take responsibility for training their employees how to be social, how to have relationships, and how to interact. Social business is not meant to be a free for all. "Companies need training on social skills," he says. Setting clear expectations (and living by them yourself, so as to set a good example) is where you can start. "Business runs on relationships, and they've forgotten that. It's hurting them," says Post. "Business has to take this on if they want to succeed."

For Post, there are two quintessential guidelines to follow, for you and for those around you, on how to be social. The first is to be on time. When you are on time (which includes communicating and responding in a timely manner), you can build up from there. If you're late (in any part of your commitment to others), you start with a deficit and have to build your way out of a hole, Post explains. "Are the first words you want out of your mouth to be, 'I'm sorry?'"

Second, Post says, "Do what your mother told you, and say please and thank you." Saying please means you are asking, not demanding; and saying thank you is an expression of gratitude. Hearing these simple words is empowering and motivating to the people who can help you succeed.

Implementing the on-time rule for yourself and others is a crucial first step. When it comes to expressing gratitude, I'm repeatedly surprised by how few people write and send thank-you notes. It's why I ask everyone at Mzinga to take the time to do this simple task. It's so easy to say thank you, and these two words go such a long way.

"Business is built on trust, and trust is built on strong relationships, and strong relationships are built on etiquette." That's why Post says success begins with etiquette. "Etiquette is the confidence to have the ability to make the choice that will help you be more successful." Etiquette, which is ultimately about being social, will help you become more successful. "Very few people can be successful in a vacuum. What sets us apart from other living creatures is the ability to form relationships," says Post. "We have to interact with each other. We'll have a better chance of being successful if we do. Etiquette is the thing that helps us to do that."

CHARISMA COUNTS MORE THAN EVER

Embracing Post's principles of social etiquette counts more now than ever, given that new technologies connect people in faster more transparent ways. This is definitely not the time to forgo manners or rules of etiquette. Devising social business etiquette for your career and that of your peers means incorporating more social skills into your business than have ever been there before, while still demanding that respect, good manners, and professionalism reign.

Why bother doing this at all? According to Alex Pentland, director of the MIT Human Dynamics Lab, social signals are an indicator of success. Pentland has studied the effects of nonverbal social cues— such as gestures, tones, and expressions—on business interactions. The more successful people are energetic: They talk and listen more; they pick up cues from others; they draw people out. Ultimately, they are charismatic. Charisma matters. Pentland found that having charismatic, socially adept people on a team will make that team more successful.

Although many of us have been neglecting our manners in the online world, when it comes down to it, we know what we're supposed to do. We're supposed to act the way we behave around our friends and family. We're supposed to be as social (and socially appropriate) online as we are offline, especially if we want to build loyal followers—either individually or organizationally. Fundamentally, this means being well mannered; and at their core, manners have always been about being socially and emotionally attuned with others.

PRESCRIPTIONS FOR APPLYING MANNERS ONLINE

To help you build your community of supporters, those people who will help you prosper, we have outlined eight rules for success that you can begin implementing right away as you build your company's online presence.

1. Pretend You're Offline

If you wouldn't say it offline, don't say it online, no matter which tools you use (discussion forums, chat rooms, blogs or wikis). Peter Post refers to the "electronic brick wall" to describe how people convince themselves that doing and saying things online or via technology won't have the same ramifications if we did and said them in "real time." And yet we've all heard stories about fights between celebrities taking place via Twitter; we all have read the Facebook updates that are no more than complaints lobbed through public space about someone's spouse. This isn't the stuff you want to broadcast.

If you wouldn't say it at work or at the gym or in the middle of a dinner party, don't do it online. It's that basic. This doesn't mean you have to hide all of your feelings, opinions, or observations. That's what is so amazing about social culture: It encourages people to share, to have a voice, and to express themselves. But there are limits. Most importantly, remember to be considerate.

2. Remember, It's Not About You

It's just not. You can't possibly be *that* interesting, so find another way to say what you want to say that engages your audience. You will get more leverage when you put others first. Too many people use social media as their own personal bullhorn, to publicize their accomplishments, their observations, and their brilliant ideas. Take a step back and imagine engaging people in a common theme, in a shared interest, or in an idea you have brewing.

The me-me-me-me attitude becomes amplified and more abrasive when it's displayed online. Four out of every five Twitter users self-promote rather than share information, according to a Rutgers University study titled "Is it Really About Me? Message Content in Social Awareness Streams."[1]

That's just unappealing. Again, think about engaging people, rather than lecturing. Instead of praising yourself, praise others. Find ideas, products, or ideas to support. Provide information that will enhance your community's experience rather than just talking about yourself. It's easy to whine, brag, and gloat online. Skip over the whining and resist the self-centered temptations; choose to talk about something meaningful, informative, and/or helpful.

At Mzinga, we tweet as a company. The marketing staff in particular tweets issues, substance, and ideas that matter to our clients and our followers. The staff occasionally will share news or insights about our company, and even some fun things happening in our offices. But no one wants to read about us all of the time. They want to read about topics that will enhance their lives, their businesses, and their knowledge, so we provide our clients with information, tools, and tips on subjects that are of interest to *them*.

---

[1]Not yet officially published, the findings were presented by the study's authors, Mor Naaman, Jeff Boase, and Chih-Hui Lai at a conference in February 2010.

3. Don't Ignore Spelling and Grammar

Social media is not an invitation to be grammatically sloppy or lazy. Yes, it is a more informal way of communicating, but poor spelling, bad grammar, and lack of professionalism only reflect poorly on you. Don't let yourself fall apart or dissolve into a puddle of rudeness and bad grammar just because sarcasm or vulgarity seem to fit neatly into 140-character tweets.

Use correct punctuation and spelling, and watch your grammar. It may sound like schoolyard stuff, but act like a human, be decent, and remember to whom you are writing. It's just wrong to treat your boss, your colleague, your best friend, and your mom the same way. Remember, what you write and how you write it is a reflection of who you are and what you care about.

Think about it: Why would a potential employer want to hire someone who couldn't be bothered to check spelling and punctuation in his or her resume? Similarly, if a business demonstrates carelessness in an email or a tweet, it could very well lead potential clients to wonder if that's the level of sophistication and attention to detail the company takes with all its work. "People focus on mistakes," says Peter Post. Make your communications mistake-free.

4. Don't Hide behind Social Media

At first, to many of us, email seemed like a great shield, the perfect way to say what we wanted without having to look the recipient in the eye while we said it. But words still matter, and the feelings they arouse still linger—and in the online world, longer than ever before. Social media makes it all too easy to spout off whatever annoyance you're feeling, or vent your anger, either through email or by posting it somewhere online.

Think you're saying something about someone behind his or her back? There is no "behind the back" in social media. It's all out there, virtually forever, so don't fool yourself. If you have something to say—and criticism is allowed, even encouraged via social media—say it with respect; and before you send it, be sure it's something you will be willing to stand by in a week.

Conversely, don't be too concerned that one nasty, unbridled comment from a disgruntled customer will ruin your business. It won't. The online social space tends to correct itself, thanks to the power of crowd. One nasty comment will be regarded as just that. Likewise, respectful criticism of a faulty product will come across as such, and you will have an opportunity to address this, and may even find that these types of comments can help your business.

5. Leave the Sensational to Someone Else

Be honest, and stick to the truth. Rumors and sensational blog posts may send readers flocking to you at first, but dishonesty and irresponsible behavior will ultimately come back to haunt you. Take seriously Peter Post's advice not to act impulsively. In the heat of the moment that sensational email or tweet might seem like a good idea. "It's so easy to push the send button," he says. Better to wait an hour or a few hours or a day before launching your message into the public domain.

6. Take Control of Yourself

Whether you are a manager or not, managing yourself smarter is important, to your personal life as well as your career. Everyone struggles with time management at some point. If work life is busy, your personal life probably will fall by the wayside; and when things are strained at home, your work probably suffers. By managing yourself smart, following these common-sense rules, you can set a good example for others from within your organization:

- Manage positively, which means being accountable, owning your mistakes, and telling the truth. No exceptions.
- Inspire and motivate.
- Recognize the accomplishments and efforts of others; give compliments.
- Be accessible and responsive.
- Foster teamwork by creating online groups, adopting new methods to share information, or using wikis to manage documents.
- Say please and thank you.
- Collaborate with your team to be more productive.
- Share and learn from one another.
- Contribute value, not noise. Resist the urge to talk just to talk.
- Use technology to manage your time better.
- Take an active role in the content you create. If someone is blogging on your behalf, be sure to continue to participate in the effort and the content.

7. Consider Yourself a Brand, and Act Accordingly

How you act is reflective of who you are. If you want to brand yourself, think about who you are, how you act, and the impression that leaves. Consider how other people will see you and how you wish to come across.

Sharing too much information and revealing personal relationships tends to cross the line in the online and offline worlds. By sharing, you provide people with something to hold on to, relate to, comment on, and feel connected to. Sharing can be your most powerful tool, but sharing too much or sharing the wrong things can be equally destructive.

8. Blog, But Mind Your Manners

A social company understands the benefits of allowing its employees to blog. Blogs are just a way of letting everyone have a voice and sharing the collective expertise of your employees and partners. When managed properly, blogging can help you showcase your company through your employees. In fact, a social company needs to showcase these voices.

At Telestra, the 40,000-person Australian telecom company, social media training is mandatory, as is participation in social media. Rather than trying to quiet its employees, the company is banking on them getting excited and being willing to participate. The company's guidelines for blogging are based on responsibility, respect, and representation. Telestra has even made the training manual available online, encouraging debate and conversation.

If you're the one doing the blogging, use the prescriptions discussed so far to guide you. In addition, consider the following Mzinga guidelines:

- Write as yourself; write relevant and write often.
- Own your content, credit others when appropriate, and never plagiarize.
- Be relevant and purposeful. Add value, rather than being self-serving.
- Be responsive to your audience and respect their input.
- Be nice.
- Don't reveal company, family, or community secrets.
- Have fun with it.

If we follow Emily Post's most basic rules, we create a positive work environment, as well as a better brand for our employer and ourselves. Ultimately, this helps us generate the results we seek: real value from our fans and friends as they follow our daily actions. We become more valuable to others and ourselves just by using good judgment. Being ethical and polite, those enduring messages of Emily Post, apply just as much to today's socially connected world as they did in 1922. When in doubt, think of Bruno and the many options you have for achieving your goals. Getting there by being considerate, respectful, and honest will bring us greater success, more rewards, and stronger relationships.

Building a Social Nation means minding your manners, online and offline, in ways laid out by Emily Post and later carried forth by Peter Post. Social

Nations are built on manners, etiquette, and respect for relationships. The leadership, culture and manners are up to you. Those are areas you control, you can improve on, and you can succeed in. The next chapter focuses on a new type of intelligence— social intelligence. It suggests that, listening, learning and adapting to the demands of others can help you build and deliver the products your customers really want.

7

PRINCIPLE 4: MONITOR AND MEASURE YOUR COMMUNITIES' CONTRIBUTIONS

A man travels the world over in search of what he needs, and returns home to find it.
—George Moore

Samuel Ganz, a Holocaust survivor and son of a candle maker, had settled in New York while his two sons, Sam and Jack, went to Toronto. On a visit to see his children, Samuel brought along a doll that had caught his attention in New York. The three had the idea to distribute the doll—and others like it—in Canada. And so, Ganz Toys was started in 1950. The company's products quickly became popular, and Ganz itself became legendary, in particular because it was one of the first companies to import Asian dolls, long before that became common.

Ganz Toys continued to grow, and expanded beyond dolls into the distribution of all sorts of toys for Disney, as well as other giftware items including mugs and even candles. The business stuck with fairly traditional products and was a solid family enterprise that followed an almost predictable merchandising track—that is until, in 2005, Howard Ganz, the grandson of Samuel, took his family and the company on a wild ride into the online world. It all started with a small, plush toy Howard invented called Webkinz.

Webkinz are cuddly stuffed animals that live and interact online with others. Essentially, the Webkinz lifestyle is the reason owners (i.e., kids) go

online, where they and their pets can enter a virtual world of fun and fantasy. Webkinz and their human counterparts can interact for hours at a time on a social networking site developed by Howard Ganz to appeal to children. The pets forge the introduction between people to start and build long-lasting connections.

For about $13, buyers get a choice of some 50 varieties of pet, each with its own personality, along with a unique access code to Webkinz.com. By entering the code, you hook up with an avatar of your stuffed animal that is ready to be played with and cared for in its virtual world. You also become part of a virtual economy in which KinzCash is the negotiable currency. KinzCash can be earned by entering contests, winning games, and working (e.g., painting a fence, selling shoes, or flipping burgers) to pay for your pet's food, give it a ride on a hydrofoil, or furnish its room.

Few details have been overlooked in the Webkinz world. Furnishings may include a stove and a refrigerator, in case you want to cook up some virtual chow at your pet's place; and, of course, you can invite other members to visit you to chat about your respective pets.

Membership in Webkinz Nation lasts just one year, after which parents would presumably be expected to buy another pet so their kids can remain a part of the Webkinz online world.

Real Insights Come from Measuring Your Communities' Interactions

Those cute little toys serve multiple purposes for Ganz. Webkinz fans—either children or their parents—can enjoy their critters in two worlds. The cuddly pets invite their owners to play with them in the offline world as well as in the online Webkinz universe. But once they click into the virtual world, customers essentially take over the marketing duties for the firm. They promote the dual aspects of the product to everyone they know, including online and offline friends and acquaintances. Ultimately, Ganz made it undesirable to be 10 years old and Webkinz-less. In this way, the company created its own nation of loyal fans and members. And to see how they are progressing, so they could monitor and measure their activities.

Just three years after Webkinz.com was born, the site was host to 2.85 million members, who charted more than 72 million page views a month. And the online social interactions and activities that were happening were keeping people at the site for a two-hour visit, on average. The company was drawing in both adults and children, online and offline. Along with its steady income from selling stuffed animals (in effect, cuddly membership codes), other toys, and trading cards, Ganz monitored the on-site ads that promote child-oriented films and more.

The ingenuity and complexity behind Webkinz, which *Advertising Age* described as "Beanie Babies on sterolds," is most impressive.[1]

Once new members sign onto the company website, Webkinz starts the monitoring process. They are directed to the Adoption Center to register their pets, choose a name (let's say, "Jake"), and

---

[1] Beth Snyder Bulik, "This Frog Speaks Volumes About Word-of-Mouth," *Advertising Age*, January 22, 2007.

visit Dr. Quack for a quick checkup. It's a personal journey not unlike one that takes place in the real world. Then it's off to Jake's room where a meter measures his happiness, his health, and his hunger. Of course, you'll want to play with your new pet and make sure he gets his exercise, as well as his special food; the animals are even programmed to tell their users just how much they appreciate the care. All of this just so Webkinz can keep track of all the relevant metrics of its community's activities, purchases and sentiment.

Pet owners are invited to keep up with the latest community happenings through Webkinz Newz. And you can chat with friends in the clubhouse via two chat areas, both designed to assure player safety and activity. In the first, players choose what they want to say from menus. In the second, they can type in their own words but they won't be transmitted unless cleared by the community dictionary. For example, "punch" won't make it through the Webkinz filter. Parents appreciate the learning aspects of the site, which provides children with the pseudo-responsibility of owning a pet. There are plenty of built-in safeguards, too, such as games that can only be played once every six hours (again, another measure of Ganz's).

Webkinz gives kids a sense of control and power over their own lives, something rarely felt offline. This powerful selling and personal proposition connects with individuals on an intimate level, while also offering a rare opportunity for youngsters to act independently, all within a community of members with similar interests.

Webkinz is a great example of not only the depth a relationship can take when a company builds a community with its customers (in this case, children). It also provides a clear picture of the value of measuring everything your community does—number of members, length of online activities, size of network, amount of purchases, sentiment of participants, and so on. It demonstrates why it's valuable to monitor the interactions of your customers and their avatars as they are playing, working, and exchanging information with each other in an online world. These social interactions enable companies, and in particular, Webkinz, to better understand their customer needs and desires that speak to both individual interests as well as member wishes within a social network. Webkinz, in this way, ensures that Ganz is much more than just a toy company—it is also a data company that uses information to make better decisions based on the input and actions of his customers and prospects.

Measuring Isn't Enough; Actions Matter More

For Ganz there is more than just an opportunity to monitor and measure the interactions of his constituents. What's more important is the potential for gaining intelligence from every communication and Interaction, and then to improve what the company does, sells, and how it responds in real time to the community's requirements. This works for Ganz, because Toy Nation of fans are always sharing their thoughts, passions, and desires. As a result, Ganz gathers new social intelligence with each interaction including emotional and social wants and needs, not just product-based ones.

Maybe you don't have a similarly passionate online community or group of customers that you are monitoring or measuring to help you run your business. Maybe you do. Or maybe you just haven't tried to measure everything everyone is saying about you on the social web—on Facebook, Twitter, and other social sites like Linked-In. Regardless, ask yourself: What if you did monitor, measure, learn, and react to the information being derived from the interactions of your customers, prospects and employees comments? What if you could use that information to help you make faster, better decisions? Further, did you ever wonder what insights you could gather from your current customers, as well as from those you don't have yet in order to determine which new products and services you should offer?

Are you wondering how this is different from listening to your loved ones or friends and then reacting to their needs? It's not much different at all, especially if you are committed to modifying your behavior based on what you hear. This is the promise of social intelligence—e.g., measuring and monitoring the actions, sentiment, and responses of your friends, fans, and followers of your company— be it on Facebook, Twitter, or your own online community like Ganz does. It allows you to take advantage of all the communications that are taking place within earshot of your team, department, organization, and company, and respond to those signals in ways you have never done before. Having the intelligence gained from what people say about you or your company is one thing, but changing to meet their needs is another thing entirely. Let's start with what it means to monitor and measure your community's interactions and why that is so important.

PRESCRIPTIONS FOR BUILDING SOCIAL INTELLIGENCE

Are you wondering where you should start to measure and monitor your fans and friends interactions? Fortunately, there are tried-and-true social monitoring technologies you can apply at your company and with your teams to get started.

Let's start by defining social intelligence. Social intelligence is the insight you receive from the social interactions and communications that take place among and between your customers, employees, partners, and investors—really, with any current, prospective, or past member of your "community." Further its about turning that social intelligence into actionable activities—new product and service ideas, better customer support, improved marketing communications and most importantly, enhanced community activity, involvement, and positive sentiment.

Once you have identified the people who have the right skills to employ and interpret these new social monitoring technologies, you can start to build social intelligence tools into your organization. Implementing social intelligence monitoring tools in your organization should be done using today's technologies. The following is a three-step process for creating a socially intelligent organization; it is based on what we, at Mzinga, have seen used by many of our leading clients:

1. *Pick the audience that you want to follow.* Who do you want to listen to? It could be your employees, your customers in your community, or potential employees and customers in the marketplace.
2. *Know why you are listening to them and what you want to learn.* Decide which type of measures and

social interactions you think you will need to listen and capture information. For example, if you host a community for your customers and you want to learn their perceptions of your products, you may want to capture their ratings and the results of on-line polls that relate to your product.

3. *Be ready to change based on the information you gather.* If you implement a monitoring system that enables you to listen, learn, adapt, and react to what you are hearing, you will be able to access useful information. However, social intelligence is successful if you can build a process that absorbs these insights to help you make better decisions.

At Webkinz.com, Howard Ganz used more traditional business methods to solve his specific problems. However, listening to what your customers and employees are saying in real time is only part of the story. You also have to be clear about what you are listening for and be able to weed out the "chatter." Social intelligence is about gaining insights in real time about people's desires you have previously not been able to obtain on a cost effective basis. But more importantly, it is about the ability to implement new proceses in your organziation to re-act to their needs so you can create loyal fans, friends and followers that help you innovate and grow.

Nothing Is Static, So Join the Social Movement Now

These three steps—Monitor, Measure, and Change—are necessary to succeed with social intelligence because nothing is static in the social world. A tweet from five minutes ago is already obsolete, but the relationship between its author and those who interacted with it has an effect that can still be measured. Our relationships not only define us, they also determine our value in the context of any situation. The ability to capture, measure, and evaluate these constantly changing relationships and the communications that emerge from them (which are clear indicators of wants and desire) help to define why people belong to social networks.

Anecdotal evidence will provide some broad, rather than targeted, insight. But as shown in the case of WebKinz.com, today's social intelligence software has the capability to capture, analyze, and respond to a whole host of additional insights and requirements. Social intelligence software can now track the following:

- *Influence.* How influential is a user or piece of content in managing perceptions?
- *Engagement.* How active is a user or piece of content in a community?
- *Sentiment.* What views and thoughts are your users sharing? Are they feeling positive, negative, or neutral?
- *Connectivity.* How connected is a user? How much reach does the content have?
- *Relevance.* How relevant is your content to the current context? Is your content current?
- *Reputation.* How much trust does your community engender? Do users view you as reliable and dependable?

These social insights are invaluable to companies as they seek to build extraordinary companies that are more than just the sum total of their products and services. As you work to build your own Social Nation, social intelligence tools and capabilities will grow as your communities and interactions grow. Most large companies have more social interactions than they can track with their current systems. This is where technology can play a role. How you build your community so that you can hear what your customers and employees are saying and respond to their communications is critical.

Thanks to today's monitoring technologies, the opportunities exist for capturing social interactions have expanded exponentially. For example, television shows like American Idol can engage viewers by inviting them to text a vote for contestants or answer questions. Doing so allows the audience to become active participants in the show. They become personally involved by sharing their thoughts during the broadcast, which in turn keeps them glued to their TVs or computers.

Viewership increases as people feel more a part of the community. Aside from the obvious benefit for advertisers, these text responses offer an opportunity to use social intelligence to gather interactions. Each text message offers an opinion or piece of data, from which additional demographics can be realized—even from something as simple as an area code.

Monitor and Measure Everything Your Fans and Followers Tell You and Each Other

If you are looking to measure sentiment, for example, you could set up a poll question to gauge the audience reactions to a show's character or plot line. Shows like *Lost* and *American Idol* take similar approaches to gauging the popularity of their contestants and story lines. Social intelligence can add even greater value by allowing you to grow this simple outreach into a thriving community that gleans insight while establishing relationships with your users. This is done by identifying the members of your audience who are most engaged in your show in a positive way, by monitoring participation and sentiment specific to a certain phone number.

Gathering information provides you with the opportunity to reach out to those audience members, to invite them, for example, to focus groups, television show discussion forums, or social network fan pages. This core group of engaged and enthusiastic individuals could then be relied on to lay the foundation for building a thriving community around your show, product, or brand. Social intelligence not only helps to establish a process that includes measures to engage your user base, it also filters and identifies those individuals who want to participate in something more.

Social intelligence can also act as your company's beacon for identifying patterns of change that indicate opportunity or risk. Social intelligence measures can act as leading indicators of change, which businesses can then act on. In the social world, perceptions, attitudes, intent, and other behaviors are constantly in flux, so filtering the noise from the truth is an ongoing challenge. But this is where social intelligence comes in: It can help you monitor and measure what's going on so you can make less errors. Hence, patterns and tendencies are revealed, which your business can use to establish a competitive advantage.

What Banking Can Learn

Take the banking industry, which is particularly interested in retention strategies for customers, especially in the wake of the latest economic slowdown. Mergers and acquisitions will continue to take place, and banks will acquire new customers, but organic growth is hard to come by in a depressed economy. Marketing is an expensive undertaking, and the most cost-effective way to stay competitive is to retain existing clients. One way to achieve this is to anticipate and understand the needs of these customers so that you can reach them before they even realize they have an unfulfilled need.

Social intelligence offers businesses the means to proactively seek and act. By proactively addressing problems, banks can retain their customers and remain competitive even in tough economic times. Social intelligence also acts as the bridge between what you can do to make your company social and what others can do for you. Social intelligence brings the two together. It's the tool that links a company willing to listen with the customers who want to share and innovate. If you already have a community, you can start to listen to all the social interactions that take place to understand the behaviors of your employees, customers, and the marketplace. If you don't have a community, social intelligence can be used to help you build one, by just listening. Either way, listening is the first step.

Social intelligence allows businesses, leaders, and others to listen and fulfill needs not yet known or met. The benefits of this intelligence range from influencing and managing the perception of your product and brand to retaining and increasing the loyalty of your employees and customers in a competitive market. Social intelligence is yet another tool that, when used properly, can help you do things differently.

It doesn't matter what you think will happen, which products you think will perform best in the market, or what tweaks you want to make the next time around when you create your new marketing campaign. Drop all those judgments, all those decisions, and listen to your crowd. Doing so will emancipate you and your business. And it will free you up to put energy into serving others, and doing so ahead of your competitors and ahead of customer expectations. Your co-workers and investors will thank you for taking this new approach.

8

PRINCIPLE 5: INVOLVE YOUR FANS IN EVERYTHING YOU DO

*Money is easy to make if it's money you want.
But with few exceptions, people don't want
money. They want . . . love and admiration.*
                                    —John Steinbeck

Adriano, Marcello, and Bruno Ducati never expected to get into the motorcycle business. In 1926, the three brothers started a company in Bologna, Italy, to produce vacuum tubes, condensers, and radio parts. It wasn't exactly the most glamorous business, but the Ducatis did well and the company grew quickly. Unfortunately, much of their manufacturing capabilities and their factories were wiped out during World War II.

The Ducatis didn't just rebuild, they reinvented the company as a maker of motorized bicycles—that is, they began selling a small motor attached to a bicycle frame. By the 1950s Ducati was manufacturing full-fledged motorcycles, which continued to evolve in design, speed, and function. Then, as motorcycle racing began to take off in Europe and the United States, the company sought to produce the epitome of high-performance vehicles.

Year after year, Ducati's motorcycles won major races and turned heads. In time, they became the must-have "bikes" for anyone who cared about motorcycles. Celebrities like Billy Joel, Tom Hanks, and Julia Roberts soon became fans of Ducati. For one thing, the $16,000 price tag for a prized bike was small

compared to the cost of a fancy sports car. Ducati fans have long had a personal (if not social) connection to their bikes and to fellow riders. There has long existed a bit of a cult or club around Ducati.

LOOKING FOR NEW WAYS TO GROW

As a way to mark the new millennium for its fans, Ducati offered its newest, limited-edition MH900E for sale exclusively through the Internet starting one minute after midnight on January 1, 2000. Within 31 minutes, 500 had sold. Three weeks later, the remaining 1,500 of the 2,000 that were manufactured had sold out. That September, the company did something similar with the 996R, its new top-of-the-line model. Despite the hefty $26,000 price tag, 350 motorcycles sold in just one day.

The company had hopes that its top-market popularity would spur growth elsewhere and among a broader group of riders, not just collectors. But to some, Ducati bikes were seen as overpriced toys for dilettantes. Worse, the bikes were known to be skittish and unreliable, and for their tendency to break down wherever parts were unavailable. The company advertised primarily in upscale lifestyle magazines, but not often, resulting in low sales, particularly in Canada and the United States. That, despite fast performance and a small, but loyal community following.

As of 2003, a year before the debut of Facebook, Ducati had sold fewer than 5,000 of its motorcycles in North America. That was when the company sent Michael Lock, a 37-year-old Englishman, to the

rescue. Lock had started out in the motorcycle
industry with Honda, fresh out of London University.
When he arrived at Ducati, his first move was a
remarkably bold one: He announced that there would
be no more advertising; in fact, the company stopped
all of its conventional marketing. Instead, Lock
introduced an entirely new social strategy to attract
interest and inspire loyalty among a larger, more
diverse audience.

To start, Lock persuaded Ducati dealers and
owners to share their passion for their bikes and
work together as a close-knit community. In turn,
they formed dozens of local Ducati clubs (physical
communities, at first) where members swapped bike
lore, organized rallies, and staged Ducati races. To
inspire and support this strategy, Lock also
reconfigured the company's web site Ducati.com. It
was integrated with all of the offline initiatives to
encourage brand loyalty, pump up enthusiasm, and
promote the latest Ducati gadgets and garb, all
featuring the company logo.

Create a Nation to Drive Revenue

To be part of Ducati was to be a part of something
unique. At the same time, Lock was making the
company more accessible and personal by bringing
together those people who shared a love of Ducati
bikes and wanted to be part of the network.

"We have attempted to modify the perception that
we are unapproachable, arrogant, and superior. The
central goal has been to make Ducati more
approachable and more human," he said. In today's
terms, we'd call this more emotive, more personal,
and much more social.

One hurdle Lock and his colleagues had to clear was the rising cost of Ducati's bikes. To some extent, this was a reflection of currency exchanges, which put the North American operation at a major disadvantage. "Our price premium in Europe was about 25 percent over the mass market," Lock explained. "Our price premium in America was 75 percent over the mass market." So Lock reduced the profit margin, partnered with dealers to do the same, and cut the price of the top-of-the-line 1098 model to $14,995.

Not content to stop there, Lock kept pushing the company in a social direction based on community input. In 2007, Ducati launched a new Monster series for North America. The starting price point for the line was $7,795, proving once and for all that the company wasn't just in the business of high-priced motorcycles. With a fully exposed engine and frame, the Monster became a quick hit. Light and low-slung, it's even a favorite among women, an emerging segment of the motorcycle world. (Ducati had also been working to appeal to female riders and was seeking to build relationships with other new and expanding customer bases.)

But the key to Ducati's new strategy in North America was to focus on mobilizing existing customers and inspire new ones to connect with the wider group of bike enthusiasts. All to build a nation of Ducati bike riders. At that time, the concept was rather revolutionary, and Lock had to find his own way. Among the company's first moves in this direction was to redraw its organizational chart to put the emerging community of Ducati loyalists at the center, surrounded by such departments as

Events & Fairs, Ducati.com, The Factory Experience, The Creative Center, and The Club.

Center Your Business around Your Community

This sent a strong signal that the company was centered around community members, their needs, feedback, and conversations. But Lock knew that he couldn't sustain a community without content. So he made sure plenty of content was available, including announcements of rallies, races, parties, bike shows, and online events. Items from clothing to bike accessories were produced, as well, and the community continued to grow online and offline.

Today, Ducati aficionados can download promotions, brochures, bike sounds, and movies through the community. They can comment and discuss what is on the site, proudly post pictures of their own bikes and race results, as well as plan gatherings. Community-generated activities include customer suggestions for new models and designs— a feature that gives Ducati's designers priceless insights about current and future buyers. In addition, members blog, discuss, and chat obsessively about Ducati's design details, new products, and races. Under Lock's direction, the relationship with the Ducati community has become ever more comprehensive. Members are encouraged to have a voice and are invited to share both complaints and compliments.

Ducati's commitment to its fans and followers is not limited just to the Internet. The company supported the formation of 59 independent Ducati clubs worldwide. Each runs its own events and newsletter, yet, in effect, all roads lead to Bologna. Club presidents visit company headquarters for a week every year, to discuss promotions, marketing, events, future products, and other issues with Ducati executives.

Don't Forget Your Offline Communities

Lock also supports community-based promotions to drive his new strategy. For example, Ducati was highly visible at the 2007 Red Bull U.S. Grand Prix Moto race in Laguna Beach, California. The company spent $500,000 to set up "Ducati Island," a pit stop offering assorted refreshments, gear checks, parking privileges, and, of course, Ducati clothing and accessories. There were even autograph sessions with the Ducati racing team. Similarly, "Ducati Village" draws thousands of bikers annually at the AMA Championship race during annual Bike Week at Daytona Beach, Florida.

All of these efforts in online and offline community building paid off. Within three years, Lock had boosted annual sales by 60 percent in North America, making Ducati the fastest-growing motorcycle brand in North America. Ducati.com pulsed with news of the latest models, awards, events, and, most importantly, community conversations.

Although Ducati was always about selling a physical product, Lock understood that the company needed to connect personally and emotively with its clients and prospects. To him, success in the motorcycle business couldn't rest only on the ability to build extraordinary bikes. Rather, it had to also be about the people who ride them and their desire "to belong."

Ducati's executives understand that it is hard to design a good company; doing so requires good products, good people, good technologies, and good processes. A great company is even harder to develop. And a truly amazing company requires socially connecting constituencies so that people are emotionally connected to one another, and to you. In a truly social (i.e., extraordinary) company, the community takes pride of authorship and ownership along with you. They become the community that can help you design and develop everything you do—be it marketing campaigns, product offerings, customer support and employee recruitment programs, or services. They become the core of what produces truly enduring value.

PRESCRIPTIONS FOR DERIVING VALUE FROM YOUR FANS

Michael Lock nailed his sales problem by making social interactions with the company's followers the centerpiece of Ducati. He did it by applying a set of prescriptions that we've seen work for many companies in today's Social Nation. Whether Lock knew it or not, he was sticking to seven reliable, and repeatable, steps to ensure that his company produced measurable results.

To start, Ducati established clear, community-centered objectives that had short , medium-, and long-term goals for social strategy initiatives. Second, Lock knew his audience, and made sure that everyone at the company continued to get to know them. Third, he determined the content that the company could and would offer. And, fourth, Ducati facilitated interactions and community, but never tried to control it.

In that vein, the company supported open communications among its customers, partners, and prospects that were personal and authentic. The company relied on technology to enable all of these transactions, while always remembering to use them to meet the needs of others. Ultimately, the focus was on others, rather than Lock or the company.

Let's look more closely at how Lock designed a social organization from which Ducati, its dealers, and customers benefited.

1. Establish Clear, Community-Centered Objectives

Defining your objectives can be both the simplest and most difficult task. If your company is like most, you have a million problems to address each day, and there is always someone, somewhere, who will gladly offer the solution to each of them. To be successful, you must be focused. Think big, and then take small, manageable, attainable steps to reach your destination.

Michael Lock's primary objective was a simple one: He wanted more people to buy more Ducati motorcycles. In order to achieve this he knew that he needed to do two things: (1) eliminate the perception that Ducati made only "toys" for the rich, while (2) creating personal connections both among and between existing and potential customers, in order to create a larger following among bikers. Knowing this allowed him to focus all of his efforts in a single direction.

Lock followed a phased three-step strategy:

1. First, he gathered stories from customers and dealers to make Ducati a community, not just a

bike manufacturer. He was making Ducati more personal.
2. Then he worked on ways to engage his audience based on those stories.
3. Next, he listened to the Ducati community to figure out what they wanted—and then he gave it to them.

In your plans to make your company social, your objectives should be just as straightforward. If, say, your main problem is flat sales, then your objective will be to drive revenues. If your problem is customer loyalty, then you will be looking to improve satisfaction and retention numbers. If your problem is that it takes too long to train incoming workers, your objective will be to shorten the amount of time it takes to get employees from hire to productive.

Yes, social connections with your customers and employees—whether existing or prospective—can help you improve your business. But you need to know what problem(s) you are seeking to solve before you get started. Once you are clear on the core problem, you can develop a clear plan for solving it with your community's support.

If you require a large audience to achieve your objective, start by building that base. If you are planning to solicit customer advice on a small product line, start by educating the audience. If you're looking to generate direct revenue from online interactions, be sure to offer great enough value so that users are willing to pay for what you are selling. Ultimately, the clearer you are about converting customers into fans, friends, and followers—so they know why they should care about helping you and your organization succeed—the more successful you will be.

2. Let your Fans and Followers Lead the Way

Building your Social Nation means knowing your customers, connecting with people and understanding your partners, and having them take the lead. You need to know more than just the number of community members you have or what they are saying. To convert your customers into loyal followers, who actually care, you must form deep, social, and personal relationships with you and their peers. Fundamentally, this means understanding what they need, and how you and the community can meet those needs, while still working together to achieve your objectives.

Start by narrowing your audience to create a base from which you can build. It's important to start focused, and build loyalty, before you expand. Consider Ducati: Michael Lock wanted to engage motorcycle dealers and enthusiasts, as well as potential customers. For each group the company identified both what it could get from that group *and* what it could offer that group.

- The dealers provided enthusiasm and product expertise. In return, they got higher levels of customer engagement and better sales.
- The enthusiasts had innumerable real-life stories to tell and needed only a venue to share their enthusiasm.
- Potential customers, who had the most important thing to offer (growing sales and revenue), were engaged last, so that Ducati could first build off its two existing communities.

To know your audience, start by defining your constituencies. Include employees, customers, partners, suppliers, investors, industry analysts, media, and even competitors. Next, think about your main objectives and clarify which of these groups has the most impact on those goals. More importantly, ask: What interactions within and between these groups will get you where you want to go? Finally, figure out what each of these groups will "earn" from their involvement with you. This is how your business can encourage members to contribute to your organization socially.

3. Use Your Existing Content to Start the Conversation

The content you collect from and deliver to your community will be important to your members on many levels. It will also be essential to your business and helpful for driving conversations. Whether through videos, articles, blog posts, or events, it's critical to update content regularly and in a way that is most appealing to your community.

In many respects, Ducati was quite lucky. The company's existing customer base became a valuable resource for information because these individuals had a strong desire to share their knowledge and interest. To facilitate that, the company gave them an outlet while also subsidizing the user-generated content with relevant and exciting product information, stories from dealers, and offline events through various international clubs. All of this content was delivered in socially enabled formats, whether in real time or online, and resulted in a growing community of loyal and enthusiastic customers and friends.

Companies often have engaging, informative content right in front of them and don't realize it. Consider what your business already has, in the form of employee expertise, studies, or original programs. A social company will enhance its existing content with both internal and external sources, and will always include its many constituents. By stating your objectives and identifying your audience, you will be able to reach that audience in ways that are appealing to all members of it while also helping your company to reach its goals.

4. Facilitate Your Community; Don't Control It

Staying actively involved in your community's conversations serves two critical purposes. First, you ensure that the conversation stays lively, on-topic, and law-abiding. Second, you develop a deep familiarity with what people are saying and how they are engaged. What's the point of facilitating a conversation if you aren't going to listen?

Initially, Ducati's interactions occurred in the physical world, and included person-to-person experiences that took place at dealerships or club-sponsored events. Today, the company offers both online and offline opportunities for engagement. In terms of the former, it's important to actively manage the digital interactions of your social network if you want them to authentically connect to each other—and to you. In order to achieve your goals it's crucial to hire a community manager specifically for this task, a professional who understands and enjoys interacting with your audience every day, welcoming new members, facilitating conversations and relationships, and meeting the company's key objectives.

5. Be Open, Social, Personal, and Authentic

Dozens of tasks and distractions compete for your attention each day; the same is true for your customers and employees. The point is, it takes a lot to get people to continually engage with your content, your business, and your community in meaningful and personal ways (especially given how many times we've all been told, "Don't take it personally"). It takes something unique to change that mind-set, that behavior.

Providing constant value, consistent authenticity, and alternative methods to engage and communicate with your community, through multiple channels, is the way to keep your audience coming back, time and again. Invitations, syndication, newsletters, Web copy, and announcements are all elements of this strategy.

Ducati did away with much of its traditional marketing, but continued to offer rich content in the form of brochures, downloads, information, and videos—online. Individual community members could access what most appealed to them, allowing them to pick and choose what they wanted rather than have the company risk an advertising campaign that never reached potential or current Ducati customers.

In the social world, communication is a two-way process. You want to provide information in various forms while allowing your constituents to gather content in ways that work for them, while then enabling each individual to use it and discuss it in an unfettered fashion. Customizing your communications can help to facilitate community interactions; and keeping these communications current will further solidify your commitment, your brand, and your engagement. This effort will also provide you with an opportunity to receive continuous feedback from your audience.

6. Rely on Social Software to Help

If you're serious about making your company social, so that it can benefit from the support of true fans and followers, you may already be using certain social tools and technologies. For example, you might read blogs; or maybe you write one. Perhaps you participate in online communities and forums. You may have started to look at social platforms for your company, or are working on a traditional software procurement process.

Before you go any further, consider this: Social technologies do not become more powerful when new features are added; they become more powerful when *people* are added. It's the widespread use of the technology that can improve your business. Of course, fancy tools can help, but you have to have something to offer, you must have social systems in place, before the latest craze will do you any good. It's more important to first build on the steps we've been discussing than it is to reach for the shiny, new toy or application.

Rather than start with new tools, Ducati leveraged the company's existing relationships with dealers and customers to build its bike clubs. As the company developed a more complete idea of the types of interactions it wanted to have with and between its people, the necessary tools presented themselves. Dealers had stories to tell, so the company provided a blog where they could tell them. Customers wanted to share, so Ducati built a forum for that purpose. Customers wanted to organize events, so the company launched calendar and meet-up systems.

Before implementing today's social technologies, it's important to ask a few questions about what your business will be doing with them. Consider the following:

- Do the software tools enable the interactions the company is targeting?
- Will your audience like, or use, these new Web 2.0 tools?
- Will your audience understand how to use the new tools?

Tools are important, but just as crucial is that your staff keep in mind that people matter more than the technology.

7. Meet Their Needs, and They Will Meet Yours

Engaging your community can lead your company in many directions, but if you are most interested in meeting the needs of others, the direction will end up leading you to something profitable and rewarding. For most community members, return on investment (ROI) is significant. They want to feel a part of a community—at least partially responsible for the design of the products and services they purchase, the marketing messages that are created, or the support they receive.

Let the members define the community they want to belong to while you reap the rewards from their commitment. Of course, this has to be managed so that it doesn't get out of control or take over your planning efforts, but you may find that your customers know better what they want than you do. So let them take the community and the conversation in the direction they want it to go.

Integrate fans in everything you do, including marketing and product development, the way Ducati did. Show your customers you're listening by responding to their ideas and comments. Whenever possible, actively promote anything your company has done in response to their feedback. You'll learn something along the way and get closer to your end goal of designing a social company in which real social and financial results are achieved.

9

PRINCIPLE 6: RELY ON YOUR COMMUNITY FOR GROWTH AND INNOVATION

I don't want to die and see on my tombstone: "He never owned a network."

—Ted Turner

For those who have never tried it, Mountain Dew is a supersweet soft drink with a caffeine kick. First marketed in Tennessee in 1948, it was christened with a centuries-old Irish description of homemade whiskey and initially marketed as "zero-proof moonshine." As of 2006, it was America's fourth most-popular carbonated soft drink, behind Coca-Cola Classic, Pepsi-Cola, and Diet Coke. Mountain Dew has its own interactive Web site, offering everything from screensavers and wallpapers to postcards and an entertaining game.

To leverage the social movement, the company established an online nation that people could join: DEWmocracy.com. Parent company PepsiCo used social media to create a network of Mountain Dew enthusiasts who would help it innovate—for example, propose new versions of the soft drink to help it stay at number four while gaining momentum in the competitive soda wars.

LET'S DRINK TO SOCIAL INNOVATION

The first DEWmocracy.com went public in November 2007. Visitors to the site found themselves watching a scene reminiscent of movies such as *V for Vendetta* or *Children of Men*, complete with dark streets, ominous music with heart-pounding rhythms, and images of corporate villains patrolling bleak neighborhoods to stifle original ideas and freedom of choice. Suddenly, a young challenger zips into the scene on a skateboard, vowing to restore the world's lost individuality by finding the salvation "elixir." His "path" is familiar to anyone who has ever played a video game; however, the choices he makes as hero in this DEWmocracy quest are guided by the visitors themselves.

Months after the launch of the online community and after a nationwide vote, Mountain Dew promised that a new, socially generated drink would "pour throughout the land"—in the form of Mountain Dew's latest addition to its product line. Everything about the DEWmocracy social-centered initiative was first-class, including the director of the introduction, Oscar-winning actor Forest Whittaker.

PepsiCo stopped short of giving the DEWmocracy community total control of the new-product development, however. The choices available to visitors were limited to a preselected few.

Look to Your Community For Direction

Still, what Mountain Dew did with its DEWmocracy campaign was a giant step forward in the art of social innovation. It is a clear example of how a company can look to its community for innovation and future direction. Doing so ensures that products and services are a direct result of what the community wants, based on what they have publicly expressed in a format visible to all. This is a far cry from the old days of focus groups meeting behind one-way mirrors.

In part, PepsiCo was successful because the company made sure that DEWmocracy.com was personal and engaging and produced fans and followers the company could leverage to drive sales and deliver marketing messages via word of mouth.

Once Dew community members entered the online world, they embarked on a journey through seven chambers, or levels, where they met mythical characters, responded to queries about their soft drink preferences, and met challenges. In other words, they played games to rack up points that would improve the chances of their preferred soda

being selected. In the first chamber, for example, community members selected a soda flavor, after which they picked their favorite color. Depending upon their choices, social participants were assigned to one of three teams whose members' selections most closely matched their own. The teams then voted on their favorite logo, label, and tagline for the new soda.

Customers and prospects were drawn into the online social nation and Web site not through traditional marketing ploys, but rather by a tempting and compelling messages using social media tools. Corporate barons ruled the city with an iron fist, yet it was clear there was a "thirst" for change. As "Seekers," customers had the chance to return choice to the people (as opposed to the corporate overloads). To do so, they had to embrace the adventure, face their destiny, and help create the next Mountain Dew. To succeed in this quest, all of their cunning and strength was required. Each chamber was blocked by a guardian and ruled by a master (sound a bit like you're the traditional organization and leadership structure?).

There were epic creatures of adventure and deception. There were enemies to fight, lessons to be learned around every corner, and tools to earn— such as a two-sided battle-axe or a coral divining rod to point the way. And, of course, there were points to be scored. The more points you won, the greater your fame in the fellowship of Seekers everywhere. (Sounds a lot more exciting and engaging than your traditional, business-centered, new product development efforts, doesn't it?) Upon the Seekers return to the city for a final showdown with the Authorities, the people were set free to vote on which elixir should pour across the land—the People's Dew. For everyone involved, PepsiCo's objective was clear: Engage the hearts and minds of its customers and prospects and reward them in ways that they had not been previously.

The company's next version of Mountain Dew was in the hands of its social network. Choice and creative freedom was the rule, not the exception. And the next version of Mountain Dew was the direct result of community rule.

Social Innovation Leads to Top-Line Growth

Creating a social network that was engaged and willing to drive the company's innovation and future product offerings was not accomplished overnight. Great effort went into the run-up to

DEWmocracy.com's community launch. Months in advance, online voiceover sites put out the call for talented performers who would bring a host of colorful characters to life, to make sure that the community game felt real and personal. The visual concepts and graphic design were on a par with those found in many of the latest video, online multiplayer games.

But, really, this was no game. PepsiCo is not an online gaming company. However, its executives understood the value of making business personal, social, and engaging. They understood that they had to do this to nurture the followers who could help improve top- and bottom-line results. This is just one way businesses can turn to others to help them.

In the DEWmocracy online community, chambers were developed and opened according to a carefully planned schedule that spanned about two months. This ensured that the DEWmocracy innovation effort was community centered, and not just a marketing ploy driven by a few hard-core gamers putting in 24-hour days to beat the system.

Predictably, there was some sniping from the more traditionally bound, but there were plenty of suggestions derived from the social network as to how DEWmocracy could be improved. In the weeks before the national online vote for which new product should be launched, message boards lit up with discussions of preferred new flavors. Conversely, petitions circulated that called for the return of the old Mountain Dew formula. Participants tried to impress one another with how long they had been Dew drinkers ("20 years!") and the role the soft drink had played in their lives ("Got me through graduate school").

The bottom line is that PepsiCo's first attempt at social innovation was successful. On August 17, 2008, Voltage was announced as the winning flavor. It was released on December 29, 2008. Based on this success, Mountain Dew announced another DEWmocracy campaign for 2010. No longer an actual Web site, the DEWmocracy community is mostly convened through a Facebook page of devoted Mountain Dew lovers. At the time of this writing there were more than 680,000 members.

In June and July 2009, before the new campaign started, "DEW Labs" trucks traveled to 17 markets in 12 states offering samples of seven flavors. From the seven flavors, taste testers were asked to choose the three for DEWmocracy. The three fan-created flavors are Typhoon (pink), a tropical punch flavor, White Out (white), a citrus flavor, and Distortion (green), a lime flavor. They were released in April 2010 and subsequent voting on the new permanent flavor will then take place.

Clearly, a new approach to innovation is emerging at PepsiCo. as the company begins to realize that their community is key to building future business and brand loyalty.

OPENING UP INNOVATION

Many companies have opened up their creativity and product development processes to outsiders. Such open innovation allows companies to glean insight, intelligence, and design concepts from people who were previously untapped and uninvolved with the company at a strategic level. This new approach—building fans and followers to help you do your job—enables internal research and development teams to benefit from the input of others.

When outside innovation is treated as a collaborative resource, rather than as a threat, internal departments can benefit greatly. In order to be successfully integrated into a company, these outside innovators have to be seen as part of a collaborative effort. Open innovation is ultimately an opportunity for all good ideas to come together into one.

Companies today are faced with the fact that it's exorbitantly expensive to find and retain talent for innovation. Many are also realizing that, while they may have the best internal departments in the world, there are still 6.8 billion people in the world, leaving much talent untapped. By incorporating, even in part, new innovation models, companies can benefit from combining external input and insight with their own resources.

PRESCRIPTIONS FOR ENGAGING YOUR FOLLOWERS IN YOUR SUCCESS

The Mountain Dew story demonstrates that social innovation can be a company's answer to slow growth, lack of inspirational products, minimal profits, and customer dissatisfaction. Open innovation should not be interpreted as punishing your internal R&D staff or having lost confidence in their abilities. Rather, it should be regarded as an opportunity to enhance and expand your own opportunities. To bring social innovation to your organization, we recommend the following three practices.

1. Tailor Your Product to Their Needs

The success of the DEWmocracy campaign began with the company's careful, precise focus on the nature of the community it wanted to create and on giving its members a voice in the results. There is, of course, a whole universe of people who drink, or might be convinced to drink, Mountain Dew. PepsiCo's marketers wisely decided not to attempt to reach all of them.

Instead, they targeted the large segment of customers who are younger and video game players, assuming that if they got involved in the campaign, they would spread the word among their peers. That decision led the company to tailor the site specifically to its target audience, which then inspired a massive flow of follower-generated evaluative content. It may sound simple, but it's also rare.

2. Create Teams to Create Communities

One of the more ingenious elements of the DEWmocracy site was its separation of the visitor's experience into solo and then team play. That worked on a variety of levels. For one thing, it simplified the task of coordinating thousands of opinions into a manageable framework.

Beyond that, the grouping of players into teams was a psychologically astute move. It helped create a stronger sense of community while encouraging interaction among the participants. The more PepsiCo was able to persuade them to identify with the game, the greater the chance they would become loyal Mountain Dew customers. The delays in opening new chambers to players had a similar effect, essentially teasing them into widespread messaging and blogging about the campaign.

3. Rely on Social Media to Accelerate Your Success

The development of your own loyal social network— as well as that of Facebook, MySpace, YouTube, and Twitter—clearly connects your brand and products to your customers and prospects. We're spent to acquire them?

Mountain Dew understands how to create an online social nation that allows customers and people to engage, vote and be a part of creating something they want and can get behind. Once you have friends, fans, and followers don't turn them over to Twitter or Facebook. Instead, engage them and persuade them. Hold on to them. As Mountain Dew wrote to its followers and fans: "It's your chance."

10

PRINCIPLE 7: REWARD OTHERS AND YOU WILL BE REWARDED, TOO

To be successful, have your heart in your business and your business in your heart.
—Thomas Watson

Some people lined up inside shopping malls, others along the sidewalks of Manhattan. What all these folks were waiting for on June 29, 2007, was the much-anticipated release of Apple's iPhone. Apple stores around the country closed at 2:00 PM EST that day and reopened four hours later for all who were willing to shell out $599 or $499 for the first two models. In Orlando, Florida, for example, hundreds of people stood in line at the Apple store and high-fived employees on their way through the front doors, cheering and clapping all the while.

Even more exciting than the iPhone were the applications for this handheld, touchscreen device. Many of them became available before the phone had been released. An entirely new industry was, in fact, born, from the 11 initial applications, all developed by Apple, to the 50 that formed the foundation of the app store that Apple had opened within 90 days of the iPhone's release. Dubbed "The Planet of Apps" by CNBC in a 2010 documentary, the application craze started by Apple has turned into a $2.5 billion yearly earnings extravaganza for the company—and that is just Apple's share of the rewards. In less than 18 months, more than 100,000 iPhone applications were designed—not by Apple, but by a nation of developers looking to fulfill the needs and desires of the Apple community.

Apple got it right. As BMW CEO Norbert Reithofer said when he was quoted in *Fortune* magazine, "Apple's customers are more than customers—they're fans. The whole world held its breath before the iPad was announced. That's brand management at its very best." (*Fortune*, "Who Does Business Trust?" March 4, 2010, by Anna Bernasek.) Building its nation of fans and followers, developers and loyal customers has made Apple the third most valuable company in the U.S. after Exxon and Microsoft.

Not only is Apple a wildly profitable company, it continues to earn a spot in *Fortune* magazine's list of Most Admired Companies. In 2009, Apple was in the top spot, earning praise from other businesses as trustworthy and admirable, for having revolutionized the way we communicate and do business with one another.

THE VALUE OF YOUR SOCIAL NETWORK CAN BE INFINITE

Although Apple already had a significant and, some would say, cultlike following, CEO Steve Jobs understood the value of building a network of developers with whom he shared the rewards. That's why he developed and released a software developer's kit (SDK) early on in the iPhone development process. This enabled virtually anyone to become a programmer and have the potential to share the rewards with Apple based

on this new phone phenomenon. It proved to be an ingenuous move on his part, as it was an invitation to anyone and everyone to participate. It was also an opportunity for those same people to benefit from their efforts in ways not previously conceived of or implemented by hardware or software giants—not Cisco, Microsoft, IBM, or SAP.

At the core of this amazing success story, which features 134,000 applications and 58 million app store users after less than two years in the market, was a simple premise. That is, build a robust social network of programmers who really care about what you do and how you do it and share the social and financial rewards with them in a simple and transparent way so that they know what's in it for them. In short, the strategy is about understanding the power of the network—people who follow you and care—and aligning compensation with your community's wants and needs.

Apple provided not only the technology framework, but also the financial incentive (70/30 in favor of app developers) to attract an enormous group of contributors, who continue to develop apps based on their individual views of the community's wants and needs. This model produced an activist community that is emotionally connected to Apple's products, socially connected to each other, and financially aligned. This underscores the value of harnessing the crowd to build a highly scalable business.

To ensure that hearts and minds are aligned with pocketbooks, as well as Apple's desire to reshape the entire communications landscape, the company clearly outlines and defines the rules for success— both for itself and for others—so that hoards of people can rally to help. This contrasts starkly with other companies that try to own everything, from the people and processes to the product, revenues, and profits.

Paying the Mortgage, Thanks to Apple Apps

Take Ethan Nicholas, who decided that he would try his hand at writing an artillery game for the iPhone. He spent about six weeks, while not at his day job, designing and programming. He was hoping that his game would be a hit, especially since he and his wife were having trouble making the mortgage payments on their North Carolina home. His dream came true. Within five months, Nicholas had made $800,000.

Of course, just like the old days of e-trading when you heard of people making $25,000 or more in a single day, there are plenty of designers whose games or applications don't get much attention. For those who do, however, it can be quite a boon. In the beginning stages of the Apple opportunity, the more people developed, the more they (and others) wanted to continue developing. The model worked and people other than those at Apple reaped the rewards.

Apps for All, Written by All

These days, the Apple Apps Store offers lists of the top-selling applications, similar to the Amazon rankings. It's daunting to think of sifting through every application and weighing whether it's worth purchasing. Still, if you're wishing there was an app for something specific, there probably is. There are applications for weight loss, stock monitoring, weather, games, navigation, restaurant reviews, and countless more.

In 2009 alone, users downloaded 2.5 billion apps from the store. In just the month of December, 280 million apps were downloaded, for an average price of $2.70 apiece. This generated $250 million in revenue, of which $175 million went to developers and $75 million went to Apple. Gartner predicts that by the end 2010 there will have been 4.5 billion apps sold, to the tune of $6.2 billion.[1]

It's all illustrative of the reach and power of a social model, one that taps into ideas and innovation in unexpected places.

Having built this community, Apple continues to share the rewards with its community, to ensure that it dominates the Netbook (small, portable computers) market. On January 27, 2010, Apple unveiled the highly anticipated iPad. "Last time there was this much excitement about a tablet, it had some commandments written on it," wrote Martin Peers in the *Wall Street Journal*,[2] about the new device. As with the iPhone, developers were already working on applications in advance of the iPad's release.

There was much talk about how the iPad's larger screen would allow for applications that hadn't yet been seen for the smart phones and iPod. Fortunately for Apple, there are already vast networks of developers and people out there who

---

[1] Stephanie Baghdassarian and Caroline Milanesi, "Dataquest Insight: Application Stores; The Revenue Opportunity Beyond the Hype," Gartner, December 2009.
[2] "Apple's Hard-to-Swallow Tablet," December 30, 2009.

have been working on applications for the iPhone. They're already engaged, interested, and ready to go. Within weeks of releasing the iPad, 500,000 were sold, clearly illustrating the power of the nation that Apple has built.

BUILDING EMOTIONAL REWARDS INTO EVERYTHING YOU DO

There is no denying that financial rewards are imperative and appreciated. Let's face it, no one wants to work for free, and few people would be designing Apple applications if there were nothing in it for them. That said, employees are often looking for rewards that come in the form of satisfaction, as well. They want to receive emotional rewards from these interconnected social networks. They seek self-actualization, recognition, credit, or some other form of satisfying emotional feedback. An article in the January–February 2010 issue of *Harvard Business Review* revealed that a study done on what most motivates workers revealed that overwhelming people want to feel as though they are making progress.[3]

They want to feel like they are making headway. Mood and motivation drop among people who feel as though they're spinning their wheels or unappreciated.

Ensuring that your employees are rewarded and feel as though they are making progress has a huge impact on them as well as on the success of your business. When it comes to these emotional rewards, we're not talking about a costly incentive

---

[3] Teresa M. Amabile and Steven J. Kramer, "What Really Motivates Workers." *Harvard Business Review, 88*(1), 44–45.

system. According to a survey of consultants conducted by Harvard Business Online, creating nonmonetary rewards boils down to the following:

- *Allow employees to have their own personal projects.* After all, you hired them because they had good ideas or are smart.
- *Let employees make an impact.* People feel empowered, appreciated, and satisfied when they can contribute in a significant and meaningful ways.
- *Help with career goals.* Showing that you support an employee's growth and desire for mobility will only further foster a positive relationship and a desire to contribute.
- *Show respect and trust.* More than a monetary bonus, people want to feel appreciated, day in and day out. Show trust and confidence and gratitude.
- *Keep people informed.* Give people a voice in big decisions, and keep people apprised of new product developments, office moves, or restructuring activities. It's easy to make someone feel unimportant by springing big changes on them only after they've been decided.

In the nation you're working to build, it's important to understand the types of rewards that are most important to your employees, if you want them to be fans and followers—not just recipients of a weekly or monthly paycheck. In the fourth century BC, Aristotle noted that people achieve *eudemonia*, a state of euphoria, when they fully use all of their personal skills and thereby achieve a sense of completeness. Abraham Maslow's Hierarchy of Needs points out that people achieve the highest sense of completeness (after fulfilling the needs of safety, food, shelter, and more) when they reach self-actualization.

DO SOMETHING REALLY GOOD

For Donna Gettings Apperson, rewards come in the form of knowing that she's keeping teens safe. Apperson is a moderator for K12.com, an online school (and a Mzinga client). As Apperson puts it, teenage hormones, angst, and drama can run high on the K12.com site. It's her job, and the job of other moderators, to watch for signs of dangerous behavior and language and threats of suicide, or even homicide.

"We are the eyes and ears of K12," says Apperson, who has intervened on numerous occasions when teens  are talking about hurting someone else or themselves. Cutting, abusive boyfriends, and suicidal thoughts are not uncommon topics of conversation. "I feel like I'm doing something really good," says Apperson. "Not only do we get the satisfaction of helping, but we get the satisfaction of the kids knowing that we're helping."

What defines self-actualization or emotional completeness will vary from person to person. A social company will identify the desired needs and meet them to the best of its ability. Businesspeople figured out a long time ago how to meet financial needs. Only now are they beginning to understand this on a more emotional, social level. Only now is the goal to provide both monetary and nonmonetary rewards.

You've now read about the seven principles for success. The next section of this book begins with a chapter that will help you find ways to get started in building your own Social Nation, as well as some of the most common pitfalls to avoid. The Epilogue covers how to become a great social participant.

PART 3

START TODAY TO CREATE YOUR OWN SOCIAL NATION

He who would learn to fly must learn to walk and run and climb and dance; one cannot fly into flying.

—Friedrich Wilhelm Nietzsche

11

HOW TO GET STARTED AND 10 PITFALLS TO AVOID

In the beginning of life, when we are infants, we need others to survive, right? And at the end of life, you need others to survive, right? But here's the secret: in between, we need others as well.

—Mitch Albom

So far you've read about how organizations are using social media and online communities to create real value, spur innovation, and use the wisdom of the community to generate products and ideas. The concluding questions, then, are how do you build a Social Nation where your constituents work as much for you as you do for them, and how do you measure their contributions so that you can maximize and drive this mutually beneficial relationship? This chapter consists of four parts:

1. A definition of friends, fans and followers;
2. The difference in value between friends and followers and fans and fanatics;
3. Six ways to get started on the path to building a social nation; and
4. An illustration of social media tools that you can use to build your own social nation (not just Facebook or Twitter).

Additionally, this chapter covers the 10 obstacles you want to avoid while building your Social Nation.

DIFFERENTIATING FRIENDS AND FOLLOWERS FROM FANS AND FANATICS

In any community, there are two basic types of members: friends and followers in one and fans and fanatics in the other. Friends and followers are those people who demonstrate an interest in your organization by following what you do and how you do it. Their interest is passive, rather than active, but they're interested enough to read and follow your organization's actions. Fans and fanatics, however, are active contributors to your organization. They add value through new ideas and peer-based support, and as sources of innovation and value-added services.

More often than not, companies that care about their communities have more friends and followers than they have fans and fanatics. Consider Facebook, which has hundreds of millions of friends and followers who post information about each other that Facebook monetizes through advertisements, versus Apple, which has hundreds of thousands of developers who create new and innovative applications for the iPod and iPad that generate real revenues for Apple.

In simple terms, this book makes the argument that to be successful, companies need to do both— attract a large group of friends and followers (e.g., the number of relationships it has) that are interested in what it does but play a passive role in its success, as well as a smaller and more passionate group of fans and fanatics that want to contribute directly to the organization's top and bottom line success (e.g., the rich relationships it builds).

A NEW FRAMEWORK FOR BUILDING VALUE

It's clear from all of the cases presented in the book that friends and followers produce value to an enterprise in many ways, including word-of-mouth marketing, feedback on product and service offerings, and peer-based support. It is also true that if you have fanatics—people willing to create the products and services for you, as they do in the case of Lynx software—extraordinary value can be created. To help you better understand the four business strategies the companies profiled in this book have utilized, we created a strategy framework called the Mzinga Social Matrix.

THE MZINGA SOCIAL NATION MATRIX

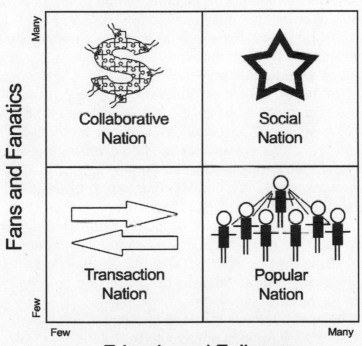

Fans and Fanatics (Many / Few)

Friends and Followers (Few / Many)

Collaborative Nation | Social Nation
Transaction Nation | Popular Nation

Friends and followers often have indirect, passive roles in business. We've seen this in the case of Facebook, which deployed a strategy of building 500 million friends that enable it to generate nearly $800 million in revenues. To help understand Facebook's business strategy, we refer to its strategy as a "popular nation." This is a company in which customers are passive participants in the sources of revenues, but the company relies on their activity to generate income.

Now take Apple, a company that relies on not just friends and followers to keep track of everything it does (MacHeads), but also hundreds of thousands of fans and fanatics to co-create and co-develop products and services that the company markets and sells, from which both the fanatics and Apple realize value. We call this business model "collaborative nation" because of the mutual economic benefit that results from the active participation of the fans in the revenues of the company.

The more traditional business strategies, the ones that most of us deal with, involve customers buying products and services without becoming friends or fanatics and without co-creating or co-developing the products and services that they are purchasing. We call this business strategy "transaction nation." Our research indicates that more than 80 percent of all businesses strategies fall into this category and that many companies don't rely on the other strategies outlined here to build active fan or follower communities to help them grow and innovate.

The final business strategy examined in the book is the "social nation" enterprise in which the organization is made up of fans and fanatics who help to co-create the products as well as attract additional friends and followers who continue to support what you do and how you do it. In essence they benefit from both active and passive participation of their community members, creating a virtual cycle of growth and innovation.

The following framework will help you think about which business strategy your company predominantly pursues and from which of those strategies it generates the majority of its revenues. (The most successful businesses would have all four of these, with transactional business being the smallest element.) This framework will also help you think about what alternative strategies are available to you as you go forward in today's highly networked world.

THE VALUE DERVIED FROM THE FOUR NATION MODELS

It's clear that friends and followers produce a different level of value than fans and fanatics based on their level of involvement and sheer numbers. To understand which type and amount of constituents you have, you need to measure all the social interactions that go on among and between all the participants as well as how they contribute. From this, you can glean insight into the behaviors of your community users and determine who is a follower and who is a fan.

For example, those users that mostly read content are your followers, whereas those users that add content and ideas, comment on other people's content, etc., are your fans. Once you can identify these user constituents, though, the question remains, "What is the appropriate balance and how do you measure it?"

The answer to the appropriate balance is that it depends on your community, on your business, and the state of your business. For example, in a sports community, you may want 85% followers because you want large, cheap (because fans are more expensive to satisfy), casual viewership to drive advertising numbers. Another example: In the early stages of an open source project, you may want 90% fans so that you can accelerate development, but eventually move to 40% fans so that you can have a sizeable followers group actually using your software. This ratio of fans to followers is your Social Nation Index, and the desired ratio describes your Social Nation Equilibrium.

Finding this Social Nation Equilibrium is a matter of gathering intelligence (social and otherwise) so that you can measure the success of your community, whether that's the amount of content or products/application being generated, or advertising dollars, or lead and event registration activity. Once you find your Social Nation Equilibrium, this represents your Social Nation—the point where your community is working for the best interests of you and/or your business. If your Social Nation Index climbs above your Social Nation Equilibrium, then your community is becoming a Fanatic Nation. If your Social Nation Index dips below your Social Nation Equilibrium, then your community is becoming a Follower Nation. As noted above, too much of one constituency over another is not a good thing, especially if your business is trying to maintain optimality at its equilibrium, its Social Nation.

So how do you achieve this equilibrium? If, for example, you have too many followers, how do you get more fans, and vice versa? The good news is that there are methods that have already proven to be successful. If you want to create more fans in your community, take a page from gaming or mobile development communities and provide incentives for innovation, such as offering currencies toward rewards, prizes, and elusive knowledge, or even financial compensation for the development of successful products.

If you want to create more followers, it really comes down to creating attractive content, products, etc. that people will flock to consume. Here, you can use reputation and financial-driven systems to benefit the strong and disregard the weak through natural selection, thus creating the most desired content and product to be consumed. Concepts like Social Proof, which use the wisdom of the crowd to influence behaviors, can help create followers or fans, depending on how you steer your users. Twitter, Facebook, and other social networking sites also have proven methods for creating both followers for tweets and fan pages in Facebook. There are a number of approaches to how you can create your Social Nation.

FIVE PLACES TO GET STARTED

As we have learned, Building your own Social Nation of fans, friends and followers to help you grow means instituting new strategies, elevating emerging leaders, and implementing new technologies and measurement systems in combination with the successful practices that are already in place in your organization. Making social pervasive throughout your company may seem daunting. We understand that.

That's why we're suggesting that you look to six different areas in your firm as a place to get started.

The five suggested departments or processes listed below are obviously not all the departments in your company. However, they are good places to begin engaging your employees, customers, and partners—in ways that they not been engaged before—starting out slowly by converting them to friends and followers of what you do and with whom you do it (other customers and partners). Once successful at that, you can begin to think about what additional tools and incentives you will need to convert your friends and followers into true fans and fanatics that want to help you build value in your organization.

1. Deliver Customer Support Via Your Community

In a social world, delivering quality and timely customer support is absolutely essential. Every business has the opportunity to connect with many communities of people. These same communities are already plugged into social media that allows them to share positive and negative feedback about your products and services. The objective here is to leverage your friends and followers using social media tools to support each other as well as you to improve their experience.

Further, if you are able to convert your friends and followers to fans and fanatics that truly want to improve your customer support, than you can achieve the following benefits:

- *Enhance Customer Support Service:* Improve your response times by tapping into the power of your entire customer base to allow individuals to solve each other's problems and answer each other's questions.

- *Your Offerings Listen to Customer Input:* Customers can learn from each other how to better use the products and services they purchased. Respond to the feedback you receive.
- *Save Time and Money:* Reduce the number of calls and emails coming into your traditional and expensive call center organizations.
- *Broadcast Your Confidence:* Address customer concerns publicly and admit errors when appropriate by letting others become your advocates— not just your paid employees. Remember, in most cases customers trust their peers more than they trust the organizations that serve them.

Remember, there are two key elements to providing social customer support. First, build an online support community for customers and prospects. Creating a social environment probably means adding discussion forums, on-line suggestion boxes, and a customer support blog to your website. Promote the use of these tools as a more powerful and efficient way for your followers to get involved while also adding to the product and troubleshooting information available from the company. Finally, consider incentives to convert your followers to fanatic loyalists customers, with recognition and rewards programs similar to what Apple does.

The second step is to act on your community's requests broadly. Address any product questions and complaints (even indirect ones) immediately so that they know that you are listening and care—or risk losing not just your fans, but also your friends and followers.

2. Build Your Brand Through Friends and Followers

In a Social Nation your brand doesn't belong solely to you anymore. Your customers and prospects are defining your corporate positioning everyday, whether you like it or not. As a result, you can sit back and let that happen, or you can make sure you have a voice in that process by engaging your followers in daily conversations using Twitter, Facebook, or your own social media site.

Building your brand with the help of others includes:

- *Creating regular conversations:* Specifically, start two-say conversations with your customers, partners, and prospects on topics that matter to them. That will get them to follow your business and enhance your reputation
- *Creating fans who will proselytize for you:* In this case, identify which of your friends and followers care enough about your organization to begin to craft and lead the conversations that drive participation
- *Reducing your reliance on traditional media:* Research continues to confirm that more and more customers rely on the advanced their peers to make purchase decisions. Consequently, reallocate your traditional marketing dollars to building your community so that they help you achieve your objectives faster, and more cost effectively than through traditional mediums.
- *Creating competitions:* As we have seen with Mountain Dew and Pepsi's most recent campaign— www.refresheverything.com people want to participate, compete, and ultimately be rewarded for

their creative thoughts. Think about what type of competitions you can run to drive brand awareness that truly converts friends and followers to fans and fanatics that reward them for their contributions.

In this regard, don't forget that each strategy recommended above requires you to build a branded community. To accomplish this you can launch a website that includes blogs, forums, surveys, and social networking tools to rally your customers. Run events, contests and games to incentivize customer interactions while recognizing and publicly rewarding customer contributions.

3. Conduct Market Research Via Both Fans and Followers

Understanding what customers and prospects want can be difficult and expensive. Traditionally businesses have relied on focus groups and consulting industry analysts, which are expensive, time-consuming efforts. Becoming a social market research organization allows you to:

- Widen the reach of your testing to larger groups.
- Engage your focus groups for the long-term.
- Expand your understanding of your constituents.

To create a social market research communities that can help you refine your thinking via your existing communities of friends, fans, and followers is essential in today's world. You can do this by launching a website that includes forums, blogs, webinar delivery, and idea sharing. Invite a large group of interested customers (50–1,000 people) to participate. Run monthly web events (webinars/ live chat sessions) describing new product and brand messaging ideas. You can begin to quickly gather feedback in the forums and idea sharing areas.

It's also important to track sentiment and product reactions in the public forum using today's social monitoring tools. Identify where the public sees negative and positive differentiation for your brand and begin to incorporate their feedback in what your product and service offerings.

4. Use Peers to Train and Develop your People

A key component of a truly social company is letting those that are on the front line train their peers the way Best Buy does through its Blue Shirt Nation. Much of the information employees use to do their jobs comes from informal workplace interactions and on the job training rather than manuals created by organization. As organizations become larger, more complex, and more geographically disperse, the virtual world of on-line interactions can bring people together in an effective and productive way so they can learn from each other what works and what does not.

Creating social training and development communities will:

- Create opportunity for "virtual water cooler" conversations as knowledge is shared throughout your workforce.
- Build internal knowledge bases for faster access to information.
- Reduce risk of knowledge loss from retirement and employee loss.

To create social training processes, begin by building an employee community. Launch a socially enabled intranet-style portal including Q&A forums, file sharing (with comments), blogs, wiki, and social networking components. Encourage informal employee interaction (vacation stories, social networking). Integrate the community activities with traditional training and learning systems through follow-up Q&A, course commentary, and course suggestions. Ask management to look for shining stars. And use the community to identify potential future leaders of your organization that you can recognize and reward for their contributions.

5. Develop New Products Via Others

Your employees, your customers, and prospects at large all have a wealth of innovative ideas for you and your product team. Embrace the fact that organizations, like Glaxo that was profiled in Chapter 1, now have a way to share those ideas and work with one another to build the best possible products and services.

Using social tools to enhance and accelerate research and product development initiatives will help your organization in three ways:

- Increase the number of ideas generated for new features and products.
- Ensure new features and products are market driven.
- Develop passionate followers and employees who have a stake in your success because they helped to build it.

In order to create social product innovation it's important to build a community in which product innovation is accessible, trustworthy, and worthwhile. You can begin by creating a website centered on idea sharing technology. And don't forget to provide incentives for participation.

You'll also want to build an internal innovation community, because your employees offer a significantly different perspective than the public. Management of the community is essentially identical and manual cross posting of content between the two should be encouraged.

SOCIAL MEDIA TOOLS TO HELP GET YOU STARTED

There are many social tools that are either necessary or will benefit you greatly as you build your social nation and constructing your network of friends and followers. This is a sampling of the tools available to you and some of the best and easiest ones with which to start. The goal is to engage fans and followers in initial conversation, educate them about your company, encourage them to interact with each other, and then maintain their interest level so they continue to engage with you. The following social applications provide a solid foundation for any company seeking to acquire friends and followers:

Social Profiles: Some form of personalized online profile (often consisting of just a person's username, their avatar, and a few other pieces of information, such as the date they joined the community) is essential in helping members establish a baseline persona, connect with other people, and form online friendships.

Blogs: Publish content to a personalized blog or to multi-author blogs and receive ratings and comments from other users.

Comments: Enable members to post and view comments related to any content, including your products and services.

Discussion Forums: These online message boards are sorted into threaded discussions, allowing members to engage in conversation by viewing other peoples' posts and responding to them to share ideas and information.

Polls: A quick way to gather information as well as engage your online audience, polls allow you to pose multiple choice questions to your members, who can vote and then view the real-time results.

Ratings and Reviews: Encourage your members to become critics (and stimulate their participation) by enabling them to rate your content, products, or services.

Converting friends and followers to fans and fanatics is critical to any organization's success— particularly in today's increasingly socially networked world—because fans and fanatics produce real value for your business: Their ideas and innovation, market insights, and knowledge of your products and services lead directly to increased efficiencies, sales, and revenues, as well as reduced costs, among them customer support. To maximize the efficiencies you can gain from your group of fans and fanatics, the following social applications are helpful:

Embeddable Widgets: These applications display recent activity or highlights from any of your social applications and can be embedded on pages within your site or other websites to increase member traffic to applications designed for member collaboration and feedback, such as ideas, blogs, and discussions.

Enhanced Social Profiles and Friend Lists: More fully formed and in depth than the basic profiles mentioned above, enhanced social profiles typically allow members to personalize their profile by arranging page elements through a drag-and-drop interface, share status updates and activities, send private messages, write on friends' Walls, and share and comment on photos and photo albums. Members can also build networks of existing and new connections by searching for and finding others, sending friend invitation requests, and creating lists of friends.

Event Management Capabilities: Schedule, promote, and manage physical and virtual events to engage members and drive continued interest and participation. Capabilities can include everything from location coordination to notifications, reminders, and conflict resolution.

File Libraries: Make MS Office files, PDF documents, and multimedia of all types available to members in one central location and allow members to share, edit, comment, and rate them.

Idea Management: Crowdsource (and capture) innovation by allowing members to submit their ideas and then vote, tag, rate, and comment on them, so the most popular ideas rise to the top.

Collaborative Zones: These workspaces within your community allow targeted groups of members to interact around specific topics, interests, and expertise using social applications and widgets.

Surveys and Assessments: Engage members in market research and capture their opinions and feedback.

Wiki: Enable increased collaboration, knowledge sharing, and knowledge management by making it easy for members to create and edit interlinked web pages.

TEN PITFALLS YOU WANT TO AVOID

Hopefully, by this time, we have shown you that the truly outstanding companies will not only create superior products and services, they will also build on and off line communities with friends, fans, and followers that can help you achieve your goals. To accomplish this goal, you must think differently about how you design your business. This includes looking at how you set up financial processes, invest in resources, and use new technologies to engage employees and customers. After all, social isn't just about a paradigm shift in technology. It also requires a business and cultural shift in how your company is organized and run.

Here are the 10 most common mistakes you want to avoid as you build your social organization.

Number 1: Running a Social Nation Like a Traditional Business

Social companies don't prosper from building their company from the inside out (i.e., products and services designed only by your own people), therefore, they must set up financial systems to measure and manage every customer, partner, and employee interaction. This includes contributions of customers to each new product innovation and the rewards that are paid to them. Apple has done exactly this.

These systems should monitor and measure revenues and expenses by community member. In addition, this requires evaluation of key financial and non-financial metrics related to each member of the community, including those that are indicators of future income (new product and service ideas), sales referrals (word-of-mouth mentions), renewal rates, and attrition related to each member of every community.

Number 2: Underinvesting in Social Initiatives and Abandoning Them Too Soon

Developing and managing true fans and followers who want to help your organization succeed— particularly in the sales, marketing, and product innovation areas—is hard to do. It takes time and patience, and needs to be repeated over and over again to create real and engaged communities. Consequently, companies need to find innovative ways to inspire early followers, who will in turn invite their friends to join them as fans and fanatics in contributing ideas and content to their communities. Eventually, this can generate leads and accelerate product design ideas without requiring the expenditure of large sums on traditional marketing and advertising campaigns, let alone research efforts.

Successful strategies include posting quality content that people want to consume, letting customers tell their stories and post their grievances, and then responding to these criticisms. Another important element is providing prospects with a place to learn about your business from other customers, partners, or employees. Using multiple approaches will reduce the cost of getting started and building a fan base. Given the variety of approaches reflected in this book, it's important to track metrics. You can and should know how many members have joined your community, stopped participating, or quit altogether.

Number 3: Neglecting to Find Ways to Encourage and Inspire Your Social Nation's Followers and Fans

Community adoption is especially critical in building social businesses because fans and followers can leave at any time if they're not happy with what you are offering them. Remember, they are volunteers to your cause, so treat them like loved ones. One of the built-in advantages of social businesses is that you know exactly how customers are feeling about you, your company, and your product or service. Harness that intelligence to meet their needs.

Since you can actually track every mouse click and usage statistic for each and every participant in your community, be sure you are monitoring and making use of this information the way Webkinz does. It's easy to measure marketing messages, test new products, and spot potential problem areas in your company; and if you pay close attention, you can use this information to drive your marketing and sales programs and keep tabs on the health of your company.

Number 4: Relying on a "Build-It-and-They-Will-Come" Mentality

Rolling out a community and just expecting people to join as friends or followers is a flawed philosophy. Marketing 101 principles still apply. That means you need correct pricing (free or fee, depending on what you are offering community members), compelling offers to have people join your community and if you want them to stay, in time, you will probably have to incent them using either financial or non-financial rewards. You also need an aggressive promotional strategy, one that includes defining your key audiences and targeting them through all available channels, to ensure that they know that you want to build a relationship with them.

Number 5: Delaying the Process of Going Social

Building your community is critical to your long-term success, given time, almost all products can be replicated by your competitors. You need to start with built-in incentives to make your communities successful so that participants will stay connected and invite their friends to your communities. Helping your community members achieve their individual and collective success comes first, meaning that your ability to recognize and reward your fans (new sales, innovative product ideas, and word-of-mouth referrals) is critical—but will come long after the initial implementation and rollout of your community.

One of the best strategies is to designate dedicated employees to act as community success managers and hold them responsible for very specific metrics, such as new members gained, member attrition, and product ideas contributed. Separate from your sales and support teams, these community leaders should have the ability to advise members of the community on how to best participate with the company and each other and generally serve as internal and external advocates for others interested in your organization—be it employees, partners, or investors.

Number 6: Underestimating the Power of a Social Nation

Another way to maximize your marketing dollars is to let your customers do some of your marketing for you. This won't just save you money; it will also improve your customer's experience and help you build trust with prospects. Remember, customers trust their peers more than they trust you.

Be sure to include customer quotes, stories, and ideas, along with testimonials, in all your community collateral, and invite customers to join your events as leaders (whether physical or virtual) to share their success stories and highlight their experiences. Use community references for every product claim or new feature—and compensate your community advocates—for helping to drive those references.

Number 7: Neglecting Employees, Partners, Investors, or Customers when Building Your Social Nation

Employee and customer communities are valuable extensions of volunteer evangelism. By empowering your community of employees and customers, you help current and future customers get the most from your product or service offerings. This in turn boosts user adoption. You also get a ready-made user group for real-time product and service test marketing, and you can reduce support costs since community members can help each other instead of calling you.

You'll find that leaders will emerge from your community population—whether they are employees, partners, customers, or prospects. Future leaders will come from places you never expected—be it in marketing, product design, sales referrals, or training. Empower every member of your community with the resources they need, then listen to them.

Number 8: Relying on Traditional Approaches when Designing Your Social Nation

Monolithic approaches to designing and implementing traditional business processes aren't applicable to doing business in today's highly connected and socially networked world. In the social universe, it's perfectly acceptable to release products that aren't yet complete, as long as you engage your customers and incorporate their feedback into future product iterations. Experiment with new, agile methodologies. You might find that they work well and allow you to incorporate authentic, real-time customer and employee feedback into the products and services you deliver.

Number 9: Developing Your Own Social Software and Analytics Solutions

Do what you do best and outsource the software and community building to the experts. Various vendors provide ready-made, complete solutions to help you build your fans, followers, and friends. Remember, Facebook and Twitter encourage fans and friends to advance *their* business, not yours. Consequently, although you should leverage the communities they have built, you need to create your own community to ensure your long-term success.

Number 10: Getting Caught without Partners to Help You Succeed

Integrating into the social web (Facebook, Twitter, and other social networks) is key to your company's future success. But as noted previously, being connected to the social web is only a part of what you need to do. You need to create a community for your employees, customers, partners, and investors—a place that is all theirs and that is connected to your brand. Given they are buying your products and service from you, investing in your company, and working for your organization, it's the least you can do for them—e.g. provide them a community they can call their own.

MAKE IT SOCIAL, MAKE IT VALUABLE

We are on the cusp of a new business era. Now is the time for leaders and their organizations—and you—to find a way to connect to individuals (coworkers, investors, customers, and partners) on personal and social levels, while enabling their fans and followers to connect to each other. All of this, in an effort to create social and emotional value for your organization. We understand this approach extremely well in our personal lives. Think about how, when we meet someone for the first time, we try to find a connection, be it over children, geography, interests, food, or movies—anything. We become human and relatable when we have a shared interest. Now, we must do the same for our businesses, organizations, and institutions if we want to build a legacy that is enduring and valuable.

Epilogue: Business and Social Become One

Life is a journey which starts at home.
—Charles Handy

I don't remember exactly when it first happened, but one day my kids turned to me and said, "You're not the boss of me." My wife and I were downright startled when our two boys, about five and eight years old at the time, announced this. Clearly, they wanted us, their parents, to listen to their needs, include them in decisions that were impacting their lives, and stop dictating to them what we wanted them to do and how we wanted them to do it.

We knew that just giving them a voice in their lives without providing them some clear guidelines would not ultimately help them succeed. We had watched our friends who had given their kids decision-making power without offering strong, clear, guiding principles to go along with that privilege. This ended up turning their kids against them. Forget fans, let alone friends and followers of their parents, those kids became rebels at every turn. We wanted to steer clear of instilling the attitude that "kids should be seen and not heard" yet prevent our kids from running wild.

ACHIEVE GREATNESS BY SETTING GOALS

To create our family nation, we began by establishing an overriding goal or principle for our kids: *Be great*. We explained to them that this applied to the three S's of their lives: school, sports, and social. Within these three overarching areas there were many decisions they could make on their own. For scholarly pursuits, for example, they were free to choose those things that most interested them, but they had to excel at whatever they chose.

When it came to sports (which included arts, music, and other extracurricular activities), we told them they could once again follow their own passion, as long as they were committed and strove to be great. One picked climbing. One picked tennis. When it came to school, one picked economics, and one picked engineering.

As for the third and final "S," social interactions with their parents, teachers, and friends, we would not quibble here. When it came to social skills, we insisted that our children be upstanding citizens who could live and excel in a global society, treat women with respect, and be sensitive to the interests and differences of others.

As I look back, I believe that my wife and I did the right thing from the very start. First, we agreed on the single guiding principle that we would use to help our boys grow into successful individuals in a global society. Second, we used that simple guiding principle—*be great*—to guide our actions and theirs, and we measured their performance and our parenting against that principle. Third, I endeavored to build a business that they would understand, and in which they could become experts, and thus could help me succeed.

I continue to believe in the simple principles that my wife, as an educator, outlined more than 20 years ago when she first identified the gap in the ways businesses acted toward their people. I now see that social and emotional talents and interactions are becoming the dominant force in the transformation of business. The more organizations put others first, serve their needs and help them achieve their goals by giving them a voice in everything they do, the more successful we all will be.

The principles I use in business are the same principles I apply at home. And they are the ones that guided the creation of this book, *Social Nation*:

1. *Communicate in the words, and use the tools, of the people you serve.* For example, we've set up a community in which you can interact—to assess your skills, share and be great. Check it out at www.socialnationbook.com.
2. *Set clear and simple principles that are enduring and understandable.* We strongly believe that building a Social Nation of friends and followers will help you and your organization succeed. We've laid out the steps for how to get started.
3. *Measure and monitor your progress and that of others along the way.* We've outlined the power of social intelligence and given you the metrics and case studies to show you the value of applying this to your business.

To prove that these principles are equally applicable at home and at work, one only needs to look at the fact that many parents are communicating by texting, which is the form of technology that is most relevant to their children. In today's world, texting allows parents to keep in touch with what their children are doing, and how they are doing, on a regular and immediate basis. Most of my friends and colleagues only learned to text in order to be able to communicate with their children. And in the last few years, you see the same trend pervading our workplaces.

Many companies fail to meet their customers and employees on their terms. Going forward, businesses need to understand how their customers and employees want to be connected and connect. We have to meet them on their terms, using their preferred forms of technologies, if we want to be relevant and in touch with their wants and needs, let alone their friends and followers who also can help us achieve our goals.

BUSINESS IS BACK TO BEING PERSONAL

This isn't really a chapter about how to raise kids nor is it an anecdote about my wife seeing the untapped opportunity at Harvard to create communities that have unlimited value. Rather, it's a personal story that illustrates how to use social media to build personal and intimate conversation in your organization in order to give a voice and control to others to help you build your business. Just as I was no longer "the boss" over my sons, businesses and their leaders are no longer the bosses over their customers and employees. Thinking otherwise is just a fallacy.

In order to build value and create enduring relationships, managers and organizations need to shift their thinking. They need to think about the people they serve, how they serve them, the technologies they need and the skills they need to create a successful business in today's world.

After 9 years of working in the social business world, I still want to build a company that has a tremendous and dedicated following of people who truly care about what we do and want to help us do it. That's why I believe personal values carry so much weight at work. My business life mirrors my personal life. The single guiding principle for my company is to create a truly *great*, social company, in every aspect of what we do and how we do it. To achieve that goal, I have translated that overarching principle into three realms, which I call the three P's of Mzinga. They are:

> *People:* Hire passionate individuals who have "can do" attitudes and who seek to accomplish the truly extraordinary in today's social world.
> *Products:* Create amazing social products and services that are cool, fun to use, and are valued and co-created by our customers and partners.
> *Processes:* Deliver memorable social interactions everyday, both online and by phone, that are positive and unique and that create value for all.

If well executed, these three principles are the recipe for our long-term business success, from which our customers, partners, and employees can all benefit. In essence, these are the same principles my wife and I have applied at home. When it comes to your personal products (kids) or maybe a community project, be sure that they are engaging, fun, and offer value. Finally, create experiences that your children, families, and friends will never forget. The rc sult? Lasting success.

SOCIAL AND BUSINESS, TOGETHER AT LAST

We started out by stating the obvious: social and business haven't always gone together. That's because individual values—such as caring, sharing, and hearing others—weren't always at the heart of business. But now, all organizations—for profit or not—are at a crossroad. Organizations need to listen, learn, and adopt if they want to prosper from these capabilities. In turn, business leaders, like parents, must provide structure, guidelines, goals, and encouragement during this social journey. They can no longer be the boss over their customers and employees, partners, and investors. That's yesterday's motto. To put it succinctly, think of your business as a family, as a community in which members can share and talk about a meaningful message, and where people truly care about other people and want to help each other achieve their goals.

Joining the Social Nation is about taking stock in yourself, through the online assessment introduced in chapter 3, evaluating what you can do to focus on social strengths, then looking at ways others can help you achieve those strengths. It's also about the glue that holds the two together. The only thing left after that is to start doing it. Get going with you, them, and the social processes that will bind friends, fans, and followers together in a mutual quest to create and find value.

The seven social characteristics covered in this book will help you establish a social business. Once you accept that business is now personal, and its success is defined by those whom you support and those who support you, you can focus on what you can do to become social (think leadership, culture, etiquette) and how you can rely on others (innovation, rewards, strategy) to get there. The results will be worth the journey.

As Ralph Waldo Emerson put it, "That which we persist in doing becomes easier—not that the nature of the task has changed, but our ability to do [it] has increased." In this case, all of us must become more centered on others, their wants, their needs, their communications, their styles, their cultures, and their requirements, if we want to prosper as individuals, communities, and societies. This in and of itself isn't new. But now we have to include business in that mix if we are to prosper, to succeed, and, ultimately, to become extraordinary. The time is now for everyone's voice be heard, included, and acknowledged in business and governments, everyday, as it has and continues to be in our personal lives. Build your social family, social nation, social community and good things will happen.

ACKNOWLEDGMENTS

We are here to help one another along life's journey.

—William Bennett

I want to begin by thanking Shannon Vargo at John Wiley & Sons, Inc. for contacting me in the spring of 2009 about writing this book. I appreciate the company's desire to build on the "We Are Smarter" book that I co-authored previously. In particular, I was excited to have the opportunity to delve into how social networks, new types of leaders, and social intelligence based on the conversations and comments of others, are impacting our business and personal lives. I also want to thank the rest of the team at Wiley who worked on this book.

I've been writing about the importance of social networking and information sharing in business for a long time, and I want to thank the people who have been with me from the beginning. Thanks to Donna Carpenter, Maurice Coyle, and my agent Helen Reese for sticking with me this past decade. Thanks to Bridget Samburg for her collaboration on this book.

As an emerging and aspiring social leader, I rely on my partners, employees, customers, and investors, to provide their personal insights, expertise, and prescriptions to help me and my company, along with its clients, to prosper. This book would have been incomplete, and impossible to write, without the Mzinga book writing team. Specifically they are Navdeep Alam, Angie and Isaac Hazard, Erika Halloran, Susan Koutalakis, Eve Sangenito, Drew Darnbrough, and Michael Migliorino.

I also want to thank everyone else at Mzinga who has supported me—and my vision—since 2001. This includes Christine Crowley, Gwen Kincaid, Robin Rose, Stephen Marcus, Dan Bruns, Mark Somol, Celina Hanson, and Randy Saari to name just a few. In addition I want to thank Howard Rubin, my oldest supporter and relentless partner; Andrew Hallowell, who has become a great friend; and Robert Migliorino, Mark King, and Jeff Samberg—wonderful and consistent investors.

Finally, I want to thank my wife Ellen, for putting up with me and for being by my side for more than 20 years while I have pursued my passion in this social industry. Thank you for giving me that initial push in this direction. I also want to thank my two sons, Michael and Adam. Along with the rest of their generation, they are showing their parents, business leaders, and government officials what the future looks like. And to my friends, fans, and parents, who keep pushing me forward despite the hills and valleys along the way, especially Ann Murray, David Flaschen, and all of my swimming and tennis friends including Bill Ribaudo, Ron Mis, Cecily and

Riaz Cassum, Ben Levitan, Dan Waintrup, and Chuck Warshaver who listen to me talk endlessly about the importance of the social revolution in business.

Mzinga Writing Team

Navdeep Alem
Development Lead, Social
Intelligence Applications
Navdeep has more than 12 years
of experience in software
engineering, architecture, and
development. He is responsible for
architecting and developing the
business and social intelligence, and the data mining
and analytics that accompany Mzinga OmniSocial.
He also designs the human and content relevancy
models and networks, and the underlying social
activity trend algorithms.

Erika Halloran
Web Design and Development
Erika has been designing, building,
and marketing successful online
communities for over ten years.
Leveraging her years of experience
in various marketing functions,
Erika manages the corporate web
site while also contributing in the areas of product
design, development, and UI.

Angie Hazard
Vice President, Talent
Angie is responsible for driving the company's strategic and operational human resources initiatives, including performance management, organizational effectiveness, talent acquisition, and compensation and benefit programs. Angie is a champion for social workplace cultures that are collaborative, engaging, and rewarding.

Isaac Hazard
Director, Strategic Consulting
With more than 10 years of experience, Isaac helps clients map their business goals to specific community and social media initiatives. Because true value in a community is generated by its members, Isaac encourages his clients to focus on delivering content and rewards to their community members to encourage participation.

Susan Koutalakis
Senior Public Relations Manager
Susan manages the company's customer, media, and analyst relationship initiatives, including award and speaking programs. Susan has more than a decade of public relations agency and corporate experience, specifically in building and executing PR programs for both emerging and established companies.

Barry Libert
Chairman and CEO
Barry Libert is the Chairman and CEO of Mzinga, a provider of social software that helps organizations make smarter decisions. Mzinga manages 15,000 communities for 200–plus large customers with 40 million unique users that exchange more than 2 billion pieces of information each month.

Libert has published four books on the value of social and information networks. He is a regularly featured keynote speaker at industry associations and for leading companies on the power of social media. He has been published in *Newsweek*, *Smart Money*, *Barron's*, the *Wall Street Journal*, and the *New York Times*, and he has appeared on CNN, CNBC, and NPR.

Mr. Libert currently serves on the Board of Directors at Innocentive and The SEI Center for Advanced Studies in Management at The Wharton School of the University of Pennsylvania.

Michael Migliorino
Marketing Coordinator
With three years experience in social media, Mike is responsible for creating and managing podcasts, videos and other social interactions on Mzinga.com.

Eve Sangenito
Vice President, Marketing
Eve Sangenito has more than 12 years of experience in the areas of direct marketing, product marketing, brand building, demand generation, advertising, and graphic design. As Mzinga's Vice President of Marketing, Eve oversees the team responsible for all aspects of the company's interactive and Web marketing strategies, including corporate communications and customer and public relations, as well as its lead- and demand-generation initiatives.

Photographs by Jeffrey Maté. www.JeffreyMatePhoto.com

Company Index

Subject Index